G000016398

Equality Postponed

Gender, Rights and
Development

Helen O'Connell

WorldView Publishing, Oxford
& One World Action, London

Copyright © Helen O'Connell and One World Action, 1996.

All rights reserved.

No part of this book may be reproduced or transmitted in any form or by any means, electronic or mechanical, including photocopying, recording, or information storage and retrieval system, without prior permission in writing from the publisher.

A British Library Cataloguing in Publication record is available for this book.

ISBN 1 872142 26 5   hardback
ISBN 1 872142 27 3   paperback

Published by WorldView Publishing, P.O. Box 595, Oxford OX2 6YH, UK.

Design and Typesetting: Tom Dyson

Contents

Acknowledgements

One World Action would like to thank all those, South and North, who contributed ideas and information to this publication.

Equality Postponed is part of One World Action's three year programme of policy change and education, 'Gender, Rights and Development'. The Programme is part-funded by Directorate-General VIII of the European Commission.

Introduction

In Bangladesh, more than 90 out of every 100 people are poor and survive on less than half the national average income. The number of poor women, men and children has increased each year since independence in 1970. Half the population cannot afford to eat enough each day to meet their calorie requirements, and four out of five people eat less than the minimum amount of protein needed. In a situation of general poverty, girls and women are particularly impoverished. In 1990, while 68 per cent of girls received some primary education, only 11 per cent received any secondary education, and 3 per cent reached tertiary level. Since 1991, Bangladesh has been implementing an economic reform programme.

In Mozambique, over 90 per cent of the population live in poverty and 66 out of every 100 children are malnourished. The 15–year war waged by Renamo (backed by the then South Africa regime) against the Frelimo government, left a legacy of 1 million dead and 4 million people displaced within or outside the country. Two-thirds of all Mozambican women were forced to flee from their homes by the war of destabilisation. The economic reform programme and recent droughts have caused even more hardship. One study estimated that 90 per cent of single mothers, widows, divorced, separated and abandoned women were unable to buy enough food for a diet of 900 calories per person per day (Fleming and Barnes, 1992: 7). Nine hundred calories is less than half the UN–recommended basic minimum. Mozambique's debt, like that of many other countries, is growing in magnitude. Mozambique has been following the free-market road to economic development since 1984.

In Nicaragua, poverty is rife. Six out of every 10 women and men are unemployed, and seven out of every 10 women, men and children live below the poverty line. The country is on the verge of economic collapse: it has a debt of US$11 billion, the largest per capita debt in the world and the cost of debt servicing is more than the country's gross national product (GNP). Since 1990, the Nicaraguan government has been implementing an economic reform programme with disastrous implications for the majority of Nicaraguans. The progress made in the 1980s towards social and economic development, and towards recognition of women's rights, is in reverse.

In the Philippines, 70 per cent of the population are living in poverty and 55 per cent have insufficient income to meet their minimum food needs and other basic requirements. Unemployment is rising: one out of every three members of the labour force is unemployed. Nine million cope on income levels which do not keep pace with rising prices of food, medicine, transport, education or health care. The Philippines has an external debt of US$34 billion and a government committed to being a model repayer. The Philippines Country Report on Women 1986-1995 (Perpiñan, 1995) talks about the 'glaring economic and social inequities and inequalities, especially in land ownership and access to resources and capital' which have disproportionately increased poverty amongst women in the last few decades. The top 10 per cent of families in the Philippines receive more than one-third of total family income, while the bottom 30 per cent and 50 per cent of families receive 9 and 20 per cent respectively. Since the 1980s, the Philippines has stepped up its efforts to increase economic growth through production for export.

Zimbabwe may not be one of the world's poorest countries but it is now experiencing increasing poverty. Sithembiso Nyoni, NGO activist and a One World Action patron, talks about 'economic famine' in Zimbabwe resulting from a combination of the 1991/92 drought and the economic policies. In 1993 she wrote: '... the present economic trends in Zimbabwe are likely to leave the poor totally incapacitated to either engage, initiate or participate, in any meaningful future economic activities in their own land.' (Nyoni, 1993).

Price rises have been considerable: in 1991, 90 kilos of maize cost 28.50 Zimbabwe dollars (Z$); the price rose three times during 1992 to a final figure of Z$105. The high cost of food leads many adults, especially women, to reduce their own consumption. In March 1992, a nationwide study showed that 70 per cent of unskilled workers, landless persons and low-income informal sector workers faced food shortages. In mid–1992, for example, the rate of inflation was 42 per cent while very few wage increases reached 20 per cent (ZCTU, 1993). External debt rose from 49 per cent of gross domestic product (GDP) in 1985 to an estimated 130 per cent of GDP in 1995 (Loewenson, 1995: 19). Zimbabwe embarked on an economic reform programme in 1991.

In the United Kingdom, poverty, albeit not as extreme or widespread as in countries in Africa, Asia or Central America, has been steadily increasing during the 1980s and 1990s. There is no official poverty line but official statistics indicate significant numbers of people have to survive on below half of the average income, after meeting housing costs (Millar, 1996). As in other countries, the gap between rich and poor is widening and women are disproportionately represented among the poorest due to factors such as lower average wages, dependent entitlements to social security and pensions, single parenthood, part-time employment and domestic responsibilities. In 1992, the gross earnings of women in full-time employment was 79 per cent that of men (Low Pay Unit, 1994). In 1994, for example, 6.4 million of the 10 million British workers whose income was below the Council of Europe Decency Threshold were women; and almost 3 million of these women were in part-time employment (Low Pay Unit, 1994). In 1996, after 20 years of equal opportunities legislation and action, while much progress has been made in employment, pay, education and social security, inequality persists in political, economic and social life.

The 20th century has seen some tremendous advances in human development. The extent of change in technology and communications is unprecedented. Computers now 'move' more than a trillion (1,000 billion) dollars around the world's financial markets every 24 hours. Advances have been made, too, in medicine, space exploration, and science. The last 50 years have also been remarkable for the establishment of the United Nations and the Bretton Woods Institutions and the proliferation of electoral democratic regimes in many countries around the world. These changes have affected everyone, but everyone has not benefited equally:

Market trader, Villa Manica, Mozambique. (Jon Spaull)

*Sandhaya Roy,
paramedic,
Cox's Bazaar,
Bangladesh.*
(Jenny Matthews)

they have been beneficial to the majority in the North, and to a minority in the South.

The 1995 Human Development Report (UNDP, 1995) tells us that the world today is richer than it was 50 years ago, that from 1950 to 1992 world income increased from US$4 trillion to US$23 trillion. Women, men and children living in countries in Africa, Asia, the Pacific, the Caribbean and Latin America — more than three quarters of the world's people — today secure only 16 per cent of the world's income. The richest one-fifth of the world's people enjoy 85 per cent of all income. Within countries, there are persistent and widening gaps between women and men, and between different social and ethnic groups. Between countries, north, south, east and west, there are sharp contrasts too.

Despite the advances made, women are 70 per cent of the poorest people, twice as many women as men cannot read or write, and girls are 60 per cent of the 130 million children who have no access to primary education. Women worldwide produce half of the world's food but own around 1 per cent of the world's land. The number of rural women living in poverty has increased by 50 per cent in the last 20 years, compared to 3 per cent for men. Women also represent the highest percentage of the unemployed. In no country, worldwide, do women enjoy and exercise their full human rights — civil, political, social, economic and cultural.

In no country, worldwide, do women enjoy and exercise their full human rights — civil, political, social, economic and cultural.

One World Action has written this book to draw attention to the widening gap between reality and rhetoric, between the lives, needs and interests of women, and men, in Nicaragua, Bangladesh, the Philippines, Mozambique and Zimbabwe, and the priorities and preoccupations of the policy-makers.

One World Action's partners in Africa, Asia and Central America are working to reduce poverty, to empower those who are marginalised and to strengthen democracy at every level. Our partners are community movements, women's and workers' organisations. Their work is a practical example of how their societies, and ours, could be organised with greater justice and equality. They face enormous obstacles: growing poverty in their communities, reduced access to essential basic services, little or no government support for their work, and marginalisation from the policy-makers whose decisions affect their lives and rights.

Added to this, what is increasingly clear to our partners is that the most important policy decisions which shape their societies are taken by international bodies, such as the World Bank, the International Monetary Fund, the European Union, the Group of Seven, and the new World Trade Organisation. In these international structures, the economic interests of the rich countries and Northern-based national and transnational companies are uppermost. It is in their interests to promote the neo-liberal economic model, to press for free trade, to champion privatisation, and to insist that the market be deregulated and allowed to operate free of any constraint; in accordance with their definition of these terms. The impact of this economic policy is felt daily in the poorest countries; it exacerbates poverty and undermines local community development activities. Our partners see that aid and loans from Northern governments and institutions such as the European Union and the World Bank are usually accompanied by conditions. These conditions are that Southern governments put in place harsh economic reform measures; they must liberalise, deregulate, privatise. Our partners see the policy statements of the donor governments, the European Union and the World Bank which state that the objective of their aid and development cooperation is poverty reduction, gender equality and sustainable development. Our partners also hear of the donor institutions' relatively new interest in democracy and good governance (legitimate, accountable, competent government which respects human rights and the rule of law) and find it difficult to marry this to the donors' commitment to neo-liberal economics.

These policy inconsistencies are particularly blatant in the areas of women's rights and gender relations — the central focus of this book. Women's rights have been on the international agenda since the 1970s with the Convention on the Elimination of All Forms of Discrimination against Women, the United Nations Decade for Women and the four UN world conferences on women, the last being in Beijing in September 1995. International and national policy statements on equal opportunities, women's rights and gender equality are numerous. Yet there is no significant reorganisation of priorities or reallocation of resources towards policies and programmes which would enable women to enjoy their full human rights, nor any meaningful sharing of power. In fact, the opposite is true. The economic reform programmes depend on, and exacerbate, women's inequality and the current unequal relations between women and men. The programmes take for granted women's unwaged and low-waged work in the home, in the workplace and in the community. They postpone women's equality.

Chapter One gives a short overview of the international declarations, covenants and policy statements on women's rights and gender equality. Chapter Two examines the implications of neo-liberal economic reform programmes for women's equality and gender relations. Chapter Three looks at what the neo-liberal economic reform programmes mean in practice in the Philippines, Mozambique, Bangladesh, Nicaragua and Zimbabwe. Chapter Four analyses the measures installed by the donors to give short-term support to people adversely affected by the economic reforms, taking the cases of Mozambique and Nicaragua as examples. This chapter also looks at women's own responses to mounting poverty, particularly informal sector work and migration. Chapter Five turns to the political considerations added to the international donor agenda in the 1990s, namely, the emphasis on multi-party elections and good governance. The chapter analyses the limitations of the donors' political agenda and how these relate to their economic concerns. The situations of Zimbabwe and Mozambique illustrate the issues. Chapter Six introduces the alternative social, economic and political vision and approaches elaborated by feminist thinkers and activists and community movements.

The terms 'South', 'Southern', 'North' and 'Northern' are used for convenience occasionally in the book. 'South' is used to cover the countries of Africa and most countries in Asia, Latin America, Central America, the Caribbean, and parts of the Pacific and the Middle East. 'North' is used to cover the industrialised countries. All such terms are unsatisfactory as they hide the range of gender, class, racial, ethnic, religious and other social divisions within each community, country and region. The terms 'international community' and 'donor community' are used to refer to Northern governments and international organisations, such as the European Union and the World Bank which give grants or loans to Southern governments. The term 'human rights', unless otherwise stated, is intended to cover the full range of rights — civil, political, social, economic and cultural.

References

Ashworth, Georgina (ed.). (1996) *What the Platform for Action Means to You*, report on January 20, 1996 conference, London, Change.

Fleming, Sue and Barnes, Colin. (1992) *Poverty Options in Mozambique: Strategy Options for the Future of UK Aid*, London, Overseas Development Administration.

Loewenson, Rene. (1995) 'Trade Unions in a Changing Global Economy: Experiences and Reflections from Zimbabwe', in One World Action (ed.). (1995) *Trade Unions and Development in a Changing Global Economy*, London, One World Action, pp. 17-26.

Low Pay Unit. (1994) *Out of Poverty, Towards Prosperity: a Report on Poverty, Low Pay and the Minimum Wage*, London, Low Pay Unit.

Millar, Jane. (1996) 'Women and Poverty in the UK', in Georgina Ashworth (ed.). (1996), *What the Platform for Action Means to You*, London, Change.

Nyoni, Sithembiso. (1993) 'Economic Famine in Zimbabwe: the Impact of Economic Structural Adjustment Programmes (ESAP) on Grassroots Development', unpublished paper.

Perpiñan, Sister Mary Soledad. (1995) *The Philippines Country Report on Women 1986-1995*, Manila, Third World Movement Against the Exploitation of Women.

UNDP. (1995) *The Human Development Report 1995*, Oxford and New York, Oxford University Press.

World Bank. (1994) *Enhancing Women's Participation in Economic Development*, a World Bank policy paper, Washington, World Bank.

Zimbabwe Congress of Trade Unions. (1993) 'The Effects of Structural Adjustment on the Workforce in Zimbabwe', paper presented by Nicholas E. Mudzengerere, Acting Secretary General of ZCTU to Winter School on 'The Social Implications of Structural Adjustment Programmes in Southern Africa', University of Zimbabwe, June 7-22.

1. Fine Words

'Women's rights are human rights' (*Paragraph 14 of the Beijing Declaration, agreed at the United Nations Fourth World Conference on Women, September 1995*).

'The full realisation of all human rights and fundamental freedoms of all women is essential for the empowerment of women. While the significance of national and regional particularities and various historical, cultural and religious backgrounds must be borne in mind, it is the duty of States, regardless of their political, economic and cultural systems, to promote and protect all human rights and fundamental freedoms.' (*Paragraph 9, Beijing Platform for Action, agreed at the United Nations Fourth World Conference on Women, September 1995*).

The 20th century saw the elaboration of codes of human rights. The Universal Declaration of Human Rights set out guiding principles on human rights in 1948. This was followed in 1966 by the legally binding Covenants on Civil and Political Rights and on Social, Economic and Cultural Rights, which came into force in 1976. In 1979, the United Nations (UN) Convention on the Elimination of All Forms of Discrimination against Women (CEDAW) was adopted. The UN Declaration on Violence against Women in the Family was adopted in 1989 and followed in 1993 by the UN Declaration on Violence against Women. The UN Convention on the Rights of the Child was adopted in 1990.

Although far from achieving universal recognition in principle, and even further from securing universal recognition in practice, these conventions and declarations are important in setting international standards. They place obligations on individual governments in respect of their structures and citizens; they also place obligations on Northern donor governments in respect of their official development assistance and cooperation. Where reporting and monitoring processes exist, as with CEDAW, these provide a useful incentive to action.

Convention on the Elimination of All Forms of Discrimination against Women

On December 18, 1979, the Convention on the Elimination of All Forms of Discrimination Against Women (CEDAW) was adopted and opened for signature, ratification and accession by the United Nations General Assembly. It entered into force on September 3, 1981. By January 1996, 149 countries had ratified the convention. The United States remains one of the most notable exceptions. Significantly more reservations (over 80) have been lodged against this than against any other UN convention; some of these reservations have subsequently been lifted.

CEDAW (1979) defines what is meant by discrimination:

'... the term "discrimination against women" shall mean any distinction, exclusion or restriction made on the basis of sex which has the effect or purpose of impairing or nullifying the recognition, enjoyment or exercise by women, irrespective of their marital status, on a basis of equality of men and women, of human rights and funda-

Organiser, National Federation of Sugar Workers, Negros, the Philippines. (Andy Rutherford/ One World Action)

mental freedoms in the political, social, economic and cultural life of their countries.' (Article 1)

CEDAW recognises that discrimination against women 'violates the principles of equality of rights and respect for human dignity', and is an obstacle to the participation of women, on equal terms with men in all aspects of life. It lists a range of measures which states ratifying the convention should adopt in education, public and political life, employment, health care, social security, and in their constitutions and laws. Implementation of equality measures, of course, remains at the discretion of each state but those who ratify the convention commit themselves to regular reporting to the CEDAW Committee which meets annually to consider progress; each country reports at least once every four years.

The 1989 UN Declaration on Violence Against Women in the Family and the 1993 UN Declaration on Violence Against Women are important additions to the international statements on women's rights. The use of violence by men against women in the family was deemed 'coercive' in the former. The 1993 Declaration took a much broader analysis of gender-based violence which, it states, 'is a form of discrimination which seriously inhibits women's ability to enjoy rights and freedoms on a basis of equality with men'.

The Beijing Conference
The United Nations Fourth World Conference on Women, which took place in Beijing in September 1995, was the culmination of a long process of regional and international preparatory conferences. Under the broad banner of 'Equality, Development and Peace', 12 themes were discussed in the Beijing Conference process:

- poverty
- education and training
- health
- violence against women
- armed conflict
- the economy
- power and decision-making
- institutional mechanisms to promote the advancement of women
- human rights of women
- media
- environment
- the girl child.

The Beijing Declaration and Platform for Action, agreed at the conference, built on the earlier agreements made at the 1992 Conference on Environment and Development, the

1993 Conference on Human Rights, the 1994 International Conference on Population and Development, and the 1995 World Summit for Social Development. The Beijing documents make strong statements about the human rights of women and the responsibilities of governments who must 'not only refrain from violating ... but must work actively to promote and protect these rights'. The documents include a very detailed overview of the poverty and inequality women experience worldwide, together with precise recommendations for action on the part of governments, international institutions and non-governmental organisations (NGOs). If fully implemented, the Beijing recommendations would improve the lives of millions of women, men and children.

However, while the description of poverty and inequality is clear, the strategy for change is less convincing. The basic tenet is that everything will be fine for all women if/when they can gain better or equal access to economic resources, and equal representation in economic and political decision-making. There is no recognition of the structural inequalities inherent in the way our societies, economies and political systems operate. There is no overt recognition either that gender equality requires a fundamental change in the power relations between women and men, that is, a redistribution of power towards women and away from men.

International Responses

The richest governments in the international community of countries have a dual responsibility in respect of women's human rights: responsibility to their own women citizens, and responsibility to women in countries to which they give aid, with which they trade, and which are affected by their foreign and economic policies.

In July 1994, the World Bank published a policy paper on women and gender and development, entitled *Enhancing Women's Participation in Economic Development*. The paper acknowledges that, compared to men, women are disadvantaged in health, education and employment and argues that positive action is required to close this 'gender-gap'. The World Bank commits itself to integrating gender issues into the mainstream of its activities and emphasises the importance of 'investing' in girls and women by improving their access to education, health, employment in the formal sector and credit. It also commits itself to 'expanding women's options in agriculture' (World Bank, 1994: 39). The Bank sees many 'pay-offs' from 'investing in women'. In its view, enhancing women's participation in economic development reduces poverty, promotes economic growth, improves child survival and overall family health, and reduces fertility

(World Bank, 1994: 22–28). There is a fleeting reference only to social justice for women as a desirable objective in itself. As will be seen in the following chapters of this book, the World Bank's economic policies, which always take priority, presume and reinforce inequality in gender relations.

The Development Assistance Committee of the Organisation for Economic Cooperation and Development (OECD) — which includes all the major donors — adopted a strong position at a high–level meeting in May 1995. Entitled *Gender Equality: Moving Towards Sustainable, People-centred Development*, the position statement asserts that 'to achieve sustainable, people-centred development, progress towards equality in the roles of women and men is essential'. While recognising that 'specific efforts to enhance the role of women in development remain as necessary as ever' it calls for a widening of the focus 'on both women's and men's roles, their responsibilities, needs, access to resources and decision-making as well as on the social relations between women and men' (OECD, 1995). It points to the importance of including issues relating to gender and women in development in policy dialogue on major concerns such as economic restructuring, participatory development, good governance, human rights, capacity-building and the follow-up to the international conferences. A Gender Plan sets out the steps, timetables, responsibilities, resources and time commitments for putting this policy into practice.

On December 20, 1995, the European Union (EU) agreed its first ever comprehensive policy statement on gender and development, *Integrating Gender Issues in Development Cooperation*. The policy calls for the 'mainstreaming' of gender analysis throughout the development cooperation activities of the European Commission and EU member states. In other words, the assumptions and predicted outcomes of each development cooperation activity must be analysed to identify the implications for women's and men's social, economic and political position vis à vis each other, and this analysis used to shape each activity from initial conception, through appraisal, design, implementation, monitoring and evaluation. The policy acknowledges the fact that the unequal division of rights, roles and responsibilities between women and men means that all development cooperation and humanitarian relief activities, from technical cooperation, project and programme aid, through to food aid and emergency assistance, affect women differently from men.

The new gender policy states that development cooperation must encourage and support changes in attitudes, structures and mechanisms at every level to reduce gender inequalities, to ensure political power-sharing, women's economic empowerment, and women's equal access to and control over social development opportunities. The policy calls for special attention to be given to positive action to counter major gender disparities.

*Fisherwoman,
Mocambique da Praia,
Mozambique.*
(Jenny Matthews)

While recognising the linkages between development cooperation and such policy areas as human rights, democratisation, and macro-economic analysis and interventions, the gender policy does not address the critical issue of how the commitment to gender equality shapes other policies, such as trade and agriculture. Article 130v of the 1992 Maastricht Treaty states that the European Union 'shall take account of [development cooperation] objectives in the policies that it implements which are likely to affect developing countries' namely, it shall 'ensure the consistency of its external activities as a whole, that is, in external relations, security, economic policies'. The principles and common objectives which the European Union regards as fundamental to Europeans — namely democracy, transparency, subsidiarity and solidarity, and a commitment to equality between women and men — should also guide and inspire the European Union's external economic and political relations.

In the final analysis, the EU's policy on integrating gender issues in development cooperation can only succeed when development cooperation and other policies are coherent with the priorities and plans of women, and their communities, in Southern and Northern countries.

The British Overseas Development Adminstration (ODA) has committed itself to promoting the social, economic, legal and political status of women and affirmed the fundamental connection between women's rights and sustainable development (ODA, 1994: 3). The British government, alongside other European Union member states, has committed itself to the implementation of the agreements made at the 1993 Vienna Conference on Human Rights, the 1994 Cairo International Conference on Population and Development and to the 1995 Beijing Fourth World Conference on Women.

Progressive policy statements from the OECD, EU and UK ODA are warmly welcomed. They demonstrate the seriousness and commitment of gender and development and social development specialists and their allies within and outside these institutions. To an important extent, also, they reveal some high-level political will within these institutions. This commitment to women's rights is not evident in other aid sectors, such as emergency aid. There is little evidence, either, that this seriousness, commitment and political will are matched in other governmental and intergovernmental institutions. Donor government ministries of finance, trade, foreign affairs, defence and agriculture, for example, pursue an entirely different agenda: an agenda which is neither people-centred nor gender-aware, but takes precedence over the stated development cooperation objectives of poverty reduction, gender equality, democracy, and respect for human rights, and in so doing undermines those objectives. Furthermore, there is little sign that those in power in the international financial institutions (World Bank and International Monetary Fund) are being weaned off their belief in neo-liberal economic reform.

Donor government ministries of finance, trade, foreign affairs, defence and agriculture, for example, pursue an entirely different agenda: an agenda which is neither people-centred nor gender-aware...

Little Action

Most governments, north, south, east and west, have ratified CEDAW and are aware of the 1989 and 1993 Declarations. Many have taken steps towards removing discrimination against women, but none has succeeded fully. Almost all governments were present in Beijing for the Fourth World Conference on Women and most governments agreed the recommendations contained in the Declaration and Platform for Action.

Yet, no government is committed to ending discrimination against women. No government is committed to ending male domination. In the last half-century, measures taken by governments to promote women's equality have been piecemeal, erratic and insufficient. For the most part, these measures, whether in the form of legislation or donor-funded 'women's projects' have been conceived and implemented more as a temporary indulgence than a right — an indulgence which can be withdrawn at any moment. Governments and intergovernmental organisations have systematically failed to meet their duties to women under international customary law and the UN Charter, as well as the more recent Covenants and Conventions, such as CEDAW. They have declined, too, to tackle and correct centuries-old, as well as modern, customs, laws, practices, underprivilege, and subordination (Ashworth, 1994).

Northern governments have been doubly irresponsible. They have not ensured the equality of women in their own countries, nor have they used their aid and their leverage on the international stage to promote and protect thoroughly women's rights and security elsewhere. There has been no significant reallocation of resources towards programmes which would enable women to exercise their full human rights.

Constitutional equality, although important, can leave untouched the architecture of discrimination...

In the last 50 years many countries, for both principled and pragmatic reasons, have amended their constitutions to enshrine equality between women and men. Legal equality is important: it validates women's struggles for equal rights and access to, and control of, resources, and it makes equality a public issue. Of course, constitutional changes alone cannot end patriarchy or overturn centuries of discrimination and injustice. Constitutional equality, although important, can leave untouched the architecture of discrimination: the vast body of laws in each country which regulate education, business, employment, social security, property, marriage, divorce, and inheritance — all of which impinge on women's rights and determine women's capacity to shape policy and command resources.

Conditions for full equality between women and men are nowhere secured; this is not the primary aim of any government. In Zimbabwe, the Philippines, and Nicaragua, as in all countries worldwide, many of the more extreme gender-related inequalities have been removed in this century. Practical steps have been taken in almost all countries to enable women to command some of the resources necessary for equality. There have been improvements in literacy, education, training, health care and so on. Overall, more girls and women have access to adequate health care, and more receive primary, secondary and tertiary education; more are in management and professional positions, and more women hold positions of political power. There are some shocking exceptions: for example, indigenous women and their communities continue to experience extreme violations of their rights.

Delegate at Saharawi agriculture conference. (Andy Rutherford/ One World Action)

The speed at which the road from constitutional reform to real equality is travelled depends on the political willingness of each government to reorient its priorities towards ending discrimination and creating a more equitable and just society. It depends, too, on the strength of women's movements and their allies in other social movements. It depends, furthermore, on a favourable international economic and political environment. Even where some political will to act exists, it can be severely hampered by budgetary crisis and a hostile international climate. Governments less than fully committed to women's rights are all too ready to give macro-level constraints as an excuse for inaction.

Conclusion
Despite the advances made in many areas, increasing numbers of girls and women are living in poverty and the gap between girls and boys, and between women and men is widening. This is the crux of the matter. What governments are doing is not enough and is contradicted by other policies so that the progress gained is jeopardised. Very little progress has been made towards ending male-domination

of the powerful international and national decision-making structures. The foundations of gender-based inequality are not tackled. The ways in which inequality on the grounds of social group and race combines with gender-based inequality are neither analysed nor addressed.

Responsibility for ensuring all women can exercise and enjoy their full human rights lies firmly and jointly with individual governments and the international community — donors, international agencies and international financial institutions. But others too have obligations to end discriminatory practices and promote equality: they include local authorities, business, the media, educational institutions, the judiciary, trade unions, and non-governmental organisations.

What is at stake is equality for half of the world's people and also the well-being, happiness and sustainability of our societies.

In the next chapter we examine the economic considerations which shape the approach of the Northern donor governments and the international financial institutions towards poverty reduction and economic development.

References

Ashworth, Georgina. (1994) 'Good Government, Bad Government, Participatory Democracy and Women', in Helen O'Connell and David Souter (eds). (1994), *Good Governance*, report of seminar on Good Governance, March 1994, London, One World Action, pp. 59-68.

European Union. (1995) 'Integrating Gender Issues in Development Cooperation', policy statement approved at Development Council of Ministers, December 20, 1995.

ODA (Overseas Development Administration). Women's Status in Developing Countries: British Aid and Human Rights Policy. Speech by Baroness Chalker, Minister for Overseas Development, November 2, 1994 at Queen Elizabeth House, Oxford.

OECD. 'Gender Equality: Moving Towards Sustainable, People-centred Development', position agreed at a high level meeting of OECD Development Assistance Committee, May 1995.

United Nations. (1995) *Beijing Declaration and Platform for Action*, from the UN Fourth World Conference on Women, September 1995.

United Nations. (1979) *Convention on the Elimination of All Forms of Discrimination Against Women* (CEDAW), New York, United Nations.

World Bank. (1994) *Enhancing Women's Participation in Economic Development*, Washington, World Bank.

2. Economic Reform and Inequality

The development of Southern countries became promi-
nent on the international agenda in the second half of the
20th century. The term development was shorthand for
economic and social progress along western lines. The international donor community is united in its statements that
aid in the form of grants or concessional loans to Southern
countries is aimed at reducing poverty. The European Union
in its document, Development Cooperation Policy in the
Run-up to 2000, known as Horizon 2000 (European Union,
1992), sets the 'fight against poverty' as its overall aim. The
British Overseas Development Administration states that its
overall aim is to improve the quality of life and reduce
poverty and suffering in poorer countries.

This chapter will assess how aid, and the conditions
attached to it, meets its objective of reducing poverty. It will
look in particular at the dominant model of economic development and evaluate the likelihood of this model achieving
equality in gender relations and long-term sustainable and
people-centred development.

Aid, Allies, Markets and Poverty

Following the Second World War and the colonial period,
Northern countries from Western Europe and North America, the USSR and Japan established aid budgets and
embarked on the funding of programmes and projects
designed, at least in theory, to assist economic and social
development in Southern countries. Aid, with its mixed
motives of altruism and self-interest, became one of the vehi-
cles by which post-colonial North/South relationships were
forged: relationships which would make it easier for the
North to influence the South's development plans, retain
access to the South's resources and sometimes their strategic locations, and importantly would further Western Cold
War foreign policy interests. In return, the South would
obtain financial and technical assistance for its social and
economic development. The stated objective of aid, poverty
reduction, made it commendable to humanitarians and
palatable to tax-payers in donor countries.

Development and poverty reduction in Southern countries were widely regarded by aid donors as a matter of

economics. By producing more, exporting more, and earning more foreign currency, it was argued, 'developing' countries would 'develop' and in turn this wealth would trickle down to benefit everyone. The development model is patriarchal. Women and children featured initially only as assumed beneficiaries of the greater wealth that would accrue to men. The model rests on Western-centric assumptions about the social, economic and political position of women: women are perceived as dependants on male breadwinners. Development planners and promoters failed to see the central roles and responsibilities held by women in Southern countries — albeit not accompanied by equal rights. What followed was over 30 years of development plans, projects and programmes which further marginalised and impoverished millions of Southern women. It took the emergence of strong women's organisations and networks, the UN Decade for Women, four UN conferences, in1975, 1980, 1985 and 1995, and volumes of research and documentation to put gender on the agenda.

Poverty was, and still is, widespread in most Southern countries. Aid does assist the alleviation of poverty in many ways, and, humanitarian motivations were, and are, present amongst aid agency staff. But aid from Northern donor governments, and from multilateral agencies such as the European Union, is rarely if ever primarily about poverty reduction. Aid is linked to trade, influence, strategic advantage and resource control. As such it is a very inadequate instrument by which to advance social and economic justice for women, men or children. The percentage of aid (in grants and loans) tied to the purchase of the donor country's own goods and services is a striking reminder of the reality of aid: for example, on average between 70 and 80 per cent of UK bilateral aid is tied each year. In practice, commercial and strategic considerations contradict and undermine the humanitarian and developmental elements of aid and often reduce these elements to window-dressing or mere appeasement.

Aid flows have fallen sharply. The 1994 figures from the Organisation for Economic Cooperation and Development (OECD) show that aid from the world's richest governments in 1994 was at the lowest percentage of GNP for 20 years. Side by side with falling aid budgets are some very significant shifts in aid spending. Much of the aid available is going to emergency relief rather than long-term development which could preempt such emergencies. The European Union — Commission and member states — is the single largest donor of development assistance (30.6 billion ECU in 1994) and humanitarian aid. Of the 692 million ECU for humanitarian aid in 1995, 235 million ECU went to the former Yugoslavia and 107 million ECU to Rwanda and Burundi. Aid to sub-Saharan Africa has been falling throughout the 1990s. The directing of large amounts of aid and concessional loans to the countries of the former Soviet Union, Eastern and Central Europe has further reduced resources going to the poorest Southern countries. The EU is particularly concerned to direct aid towards its immediate neighbours, not only in Central and Eastern Europe but also countries around the Mediterranean; EU aid is inextricably linked to its trading interests and to the Union's future enlargement.

The overall result is that very little aid is directed to poverty reduction or to meeting the long-term needs and interests of women in Southern countries.

Stabilise and Grow?

The growth model of economic development reached new levels of sophistication and universality in the 1980s and 1990s with the debt crisis and the neo-liberal economic measures promoted by the International Monetary Fund (IMF) and the World Bank to deal with it and to avoid a reoccurrence. Since the 1980s, new lending and much aid to developing countries are given under certain conditions defined by the IMF and the World Bank. Without these institutions' seal of approval — that is, without a stabilisation and structural adjustment programme — indebted countries are deemed ineligible for new credit. Once an indebted country has begun the required economic policy changes and met agreed targets, credit becomes available. This seal of approval also quickly became essential to attract private

Communal vegetable garden, Northern Transvaal, South Africa. (Gisele Wolfsohn/ Panos Pictures)

investment and increasingly necessary to obtain aid. The economies of Southern countries were to be integrated more fully into the free-market global economy.

That indebted Southern countries had to make economic adjustments was irrefutable: their situation was untenable. What is debatable is the nature, scope and duration of the adjustments.

Already committed to neo-liberal economic policies at home, some Northern governments, led by the UK and the US and their advisers saw little reason why similar policies should not be adopted in the South. The significant differences in economic, social and political realities, North and South, appear to have received little attention; neither did the differences between Southern countries. The stage of industrial and agricultural development, the extent of poverty and inequality, and the nature of colonial legacy were ignored. So too were education and training standards, population size, value of natural resource base, and degree of social cohesion. Countries as poor as Mozambique or Bolivia, or as relatively better-off as Zimbabwe or Chile, were prescribed the same remedy for economic recovery. These differences were to determine the scale of the impact of economic reform on the majority of women, men and children, and ultimately in many countries to undermine any potential long-term benefits of the reform process itself. Even those developing countries, such as Bangladesh, with relatively little debt, are expected to follow the same economic path if they wish to continue to receive aid and concessional loans.

The neo-liberal economic reform package contained two parts: stabilisation and structural adjustment programmes. Stabilisation programmes are a series of shock measures aimed to achieve a balance of payments equilibrium in a number of years by reducing public and private domestic demand and reducing budgetary deficits. Supposedly, demand is decreased principally by devaluing the currency and thereby reducing real incomes, and by removing price controls. Currency devaluation has the added benefit of making exports cheaper and therefore, theoretically at least, making it easier to export. Budget deficits are lowered by cutting public expenditure, for example, by laying off public employees, and removing subsidies on basic commodities, or services, such as food, fuel, water, and public transport. There was no emphasis on reducing public expenditure on defence or the police.

The second part of the package, structural adjustment programmes, aimed to bring about economic growth through improving the incentive structure for commercial enterprises, promoting production for export, liberalising trading relations, deregulating the economy, and privatising state-owned enterprises and public services. The underlying principle of structural adjustment is that the 'market', if freed of government interference, corruption and cronyism, and inhibiting regulations, will operate efficiently and ensure economic growth.

Counting on Inequality

The economic reform programmes force women into situations where they have to work for exploitative wages in increasingly over-crowded labour markets. The reforms decimate the public infrastructure necessary for women to fulfil those family and community responsibilities allocated to them. At the same time, the economic changes remove, or severely restrict, the means by which women could achieve equality in gender relations, such as education, training, employment, and time to organise and to assert their rights.

The economic reform package concerned itself only with macro-economic matters: achieving a balance of payments equilibrium, reducing budget deficits, getting prices right, removing the state from any role in regulating economic affairs. It paid no attention to micro- and meso-level economic matters or to non-formal and non-monetised economic activities. The question of how resources and wealth are distributed are overlooked and with it the gender differentials evident in the control of economic resources, such as land, and in access to education, training and credit.

Neo-classical economics, the driving force of structural adjustment, is inherently male-biased. This economic thinking assumes that everyone is guided purely by self-interest and the desire to maximise their own advantage. It assumes, too, that everyone can sell their labour power in the market place on a more or less equal basis. However, the choices women and men make about how they use their unwaged and waged labour time are informed by gender and wider social relations. In particular, women's attitudes, preferences and possibilities for independent and self-interested action are integrally linked to power and gender relations. The concept and implementation of neo-liberal economic reform programmes depend on the existing unequal division of rights and responsibilities between women and men; they exploit the existing unequal gender contract within the household. Far from addressing the inequality in gender relations, the structural adjustment programmes perpetuate and exacerbate it (see Elson, 1995; Sparr, 1994; Bakker, 1994; Dalla Costa and Dalla Costa, 1995). Structural adjustment presumes the continuation and extension of women's unwaged work in the home, community and economy. Few women will turn their back on hungry children in need of

Neo-classical economics, the driving force of structural adjustment, is inherently male-biased.

Tobacco workers in privately-owned factory, Esteli, Nicaragua.
(Jenny Matthews)

food, an ill child in need of medicine, an elderly relative in need of care, or an unemployed partner in need of moral support.

Neo-classical economic thinking, and its trust in the market, has the fundamental flaw of not being able to take account of activities and effects which do not have a price — those that relate to unwaged labour. In every case, women are more likely than men to suffer from the undemocratic nature of market-forces. Women are the major providers of unpaid labour; women's lack of rights to property or other assets to use as collateral limits their access to credit; women's family responsibilities, coupled with inadequate access to education or training, and resultant poverty, means that women are more likely to have to settle for exploitative labour conditions (Elson, 1991). Markets do not operate on a one person, one vote basis but instead give most say to those with most purchasing power. Similarly, as Elson (1991) points out, markets exercise coercion as well as freedom: 'the person with no assets and no income transfers from kin or welfare state is forced to sell his/her labour at whatever price he/she can get in order to survive'.

The impact of the economic reform package on the major-ity of women, men and children was immediate and devastating. Currency devaluation caused sharp falls in real wages, while inflation and the removal of subsidies pushed up the cost of food and other basic commodities. Together with the introduction of charges for health care and education, the result has been a dramatic decline in household income and living standards, the burden of which falls disproportionately on women. The cuts in public spending led to reduced public services and job losses, particularly for women for whom that sector had offered good employment opportunities. Industrial workers were also adversely affected by cheaper inports following trade liberalisation and the squeeze on credit. While structural adjustment had the stated aim of increasing agricultural productivity, it ignored the situation of women farmers who generally grow different crops, often for local or their own consumption, have limited land rights and restricted access to credit, training and inputs. The fact that women are often obliged to provide free labour on their husbands' or male relatives' fields was also disregarded. Ingrid Palmer (1988) points out that the notion that land productivity can be increased for internal use or export by relying on higher-yielding crops and chemicals is based on the implicit assumption that 'more labour time can be squeezed out of women for the more labour-intensive practices which result from the increases in land productivity'. The impact of structural adjustment programmes on agriculture in Mozambique and the Philippines is looked at in detail in Chapter Three.

Women cannot exercise or enjoy their full human rights in a situation of mounting poverty and insecurity, or when day-to-day survival takes precedence over all else.

Women cannot exercise or enjoy their full human rights in a situation of mounting poverty and insecurity, or when day-to-day survival takes precedence over all else.

While the present situation of millions of adult women in many countries in Africa, Asia and Latin America is dire, the long-term implications for girls and young women are also daunting: the privatisation of education and the introduction of school fees has meant that many families are forced to choose which of their children to educate. Many parents opt to educate their sons. There are other factors, too, which operate against girls' education: girls are frequently removed from school to look after younger siblings while adult family members are out seeking cash income. The education of boys and young men is not guaranteed either: in the poorest households, all children are involved in trying to earn some income as street traders, or in other forms of child labour. In the poorest parts of the poorest countries, schools no longer function in any normal fashion: educational materials are scarce or non-existent, and teachers are forced to seek additional sources of income to supplement their meagre salaries; some are no longer paid.

Mozambique provides a stark illustration of this. Primary school enrolment rates fell from 47 per cent in 1987 to 40 per cent in 1990 under the Economic Rehabilitation Programme (PRE), Mozambique's structural adjustment programme. Under the PRE, state expenditure on education fell from 17 per cent of the state budget in 1986 to 10 per cent in 1988 (Correia, 1993: 14). Classes reached sizes of 60 to 80 pupils compared with the average of 41 for sub-Saharan Africa as a whole (WUS, 1994: 2). Writing in 1991, Reginald Green reported that many primary schools were operating a two or three shift system, which is exhausting for teachers and limits each child's education to as little as three hours per day. Public expenditure cuts have also affected health care with privatisation of services and the introduction of fees further limiting most people's access to health care. The impact on health care in Nicaragua is dealt with in Chapter Three.

Even on their own narrow economic grounds, structural adjustment programmes are flawed. Not all African, Asian or Latin American industries are strong enough to compete effectively in global markets where prices are controlled firmly by transnational corporations. Secondly, if many indebted countries embark simultaneously on the path of production for export, whether in food crops, manufactured goods or services, the price of these goods or services on the global market will fall correspondingly. Thirdly, while the liberalisation of trading relations may assist exports, it can also have the effect of making imports cheaper. In very many developing counties, the private and public domestic demand for goods and services is so low, and further lowered by the economic reforms, that local industries cannot compete. The very policies of protection, use of selective subsidies and so on which were instrumental in bringing about the economic success of the late-developing countries, such as Germany, and the newly-industrialising countries (NICs) were precluded by the economic reform package. Hypocritically, Northern industrialised countries continued to employ protectionist policies at home while promoting 'free market' neo-liberalism abroad.

Integration into the Global Economy

From the narrow and short-term perspective of the lenders, the measures promoted to deal with the debt crisis have ensured that indebted countries continue to service the debts. But the strategy has not resolved the crisis and debts are mounting. The total value of outstanding loans, including grants and loans from Northern governments, the World Bank and the IMF, continues to grow and stood at almost US$2 trillion in 1994; this represents a 7 per cent increase on

Kill VAT and anti-IMF demonstration in Manila, the Philippines in June 1994. Government was proposing to increase VAT and extend it to more basic goods. (Andy Rutherford/ One World Action)

1993 figures. Each year, African governments pay over US$13 billion to Northern creditors, more than double their expenditure on health and primary education. No serious efforts have been made to divert resources from excessive military expenditure, and there is no political will in the North to slow-down or control the sale of arms to Southern indebted countries.

The debt crisis and the economic reform process have opened the way for the further globalisation of important parts of world trade. The liberalisation of trade at the national level, accomplished by the economic reform process, has been further advanced by changes at the international level brought about through the General Agreement on Tariffs and Trade (GATT) Uruguay Round of talks and final GATT IV agreement in 1993. Average world tariffs were progressively reduced from 40 per cent in the late 1940s to 5 per cent by the end of the GATT talks in 1993. GATT IV established the World Trade Organisation to undertake the supervision of world trade. The end result has been a dramatic liberalisation and deregulation of trade and an increasing globalisation of services, production and markets in the last 30 years. The gender implications of these developments are explored in more detail in Chapter Three.

Transnational corporations and international finance companies together dominate the global economy...

Under the final GATT agreement, in writing at least, all countries have equal access to international markets. In practice, all countries do not compete on an equal basis. Seventy per cent of world trade is between and within transnational corporations (and 40 per cent is controlled by 350 companies), and trading structures are firmly biased in favour of the big players. Transnational corporations and international finance companies together dominate the global economy. Global trade, finance and credit, transportation and intellectual property rights are all within their domain and for the most part outside the jurisdiction of governments. They are the real beneficiaries of the debt crisis and the neo-liberal economic reform programmes.

Conclusion

The debt crisis and the subsequent economic reform process have put enormous strains on women's resources, energy, time and good will. The immediate price women pay is increased poverty, longer hours spent trying to earn some income, and exhaustion. The cost, too, is opportunities for equality postponed and, in effect, rights rescinded.

...they are the real beneficiaries of the debt crisis and the neo-liberal economic reform programmes.

The classification of unwaged work — caring, domestic work, community work — as non-productive or non-market, and therefore valueless, had profound implications in an economic model which to a great extent recognises only monetary values. Uncounted work means uncounted workers, and uncounted workers have little right to make demands for economic wellbeing or social security protection. The effects of this narrow economic thinking are detrimental not only to women, but to indigenous communities and other marginalised groups who operate outside the formal wage economy.

In June 1995, the European Union adopted a new policy position on structural adjustment. This recognised that in certain regions 'significant reductions in public expenditures' had been made to the detriment of maintaining economic and social, and in some cases, political, infrastructure. It also acknowledged that, in particular, basic services had been sacrificed on the altar of short-term economic stability. The new position reiterated the view that economic reform is a necessity but opened the way for rethinking the reform package. It stated, for example, that particular attention should be paid to the sequencing of reforms, to more appropriate conditionality, to local capacity, and to regional dimensions, and it called for increased participation by national partners in the definition and content of the programmes. Importantly, the new policy emphasised the need 'to take account of all the economic and social realities of the countries concerned and, among other things, assess the impact of the measures concerned on all men and women' (European Union, 1995).

Control of her body. Poster protesting the promotion of injectable contraceptives by Narigrantha Prabartana, Bangladesh.

If put into full effect, this new EU policy could transform the Union's approach to economic and social development. It remains for the EU to put its words into action, and influence thinking within the World Bank and the IMF.

The ongoing debt crisis has given the international financial institutions, such as the IMF and the World Bank, the World Trade Organisation, the Group of Seven major industrialised countries (the G7), and the European Union unprecedented power over the South — power which is much more far-reaching than that achieved through aid. The debt crisis, coupled with the collapse in demand for the South's primary products, has brought about a new balance, or imbalance, of power; the South has lost any bargaining power it once had. The collapse of the Soviet Union and the opening up of Russia, Eastern and Central Europe has exacerbated this imbalance by offering new opportunities for investment.

Aid remains an important, though diminishing, potential source of investment to the poorest countries which are unable to attract foreign investment on the open market. Aid could assist in the development of essential systems of education and health and in the provision of housing, water and transport services. At the World Summit for Social Development in March 1995, there was agreement that a minimum of 20 per cent of aid and 20 per cent of Southern national budgets should be directed towards social programmes. It remains to be seen how the international donor community's promise to direct resources to social programmes fits with their ongoing commitment to privatisation and reducing public spending.

The social and economic ramifications of the debt crisis and the measures taken to deal with it, namely IMF / World Bank-conceived stabilisation and structural adjustment programmes, are profound in most countries in Africa, Asia and Latin America. While the debate on whether increased poverty can or cannot be attributed directly to structural adjustment will continue for many decades, what is incontrovertible is that poverty and marginalisation have increased for the majority of women, men and children in Southern countries, and disproportionately for women. The neo-liberal economic reform process, and consequent globalisation, count on and reinforce gender inequality. The next chapter looks in more detail at what the neo-liberal economic reforms mean in practice for women in the Philippines, Mozambique, Bangladesh, Nicaragua and Zimbabwe.

References

Bakker, Isabella. (ed.) (1994) *The Strategic Silence: Gender and Economic Policy.* London and New Jersey, Zed Books in association with The North-South Institute.

Duckworth, Beverley. (1995) 'Ideology and Rhetoric in World Bank Gender Policy: a Feminist Critique.' unpublished paper.

CIDMAA (Centre d'Information et de Documentation sur le Mozambique et l'Afrique Australe)/COCAMO (Cooperation Canada Mozambique). (1989) *Mozambique 1989 — New Directions*, Montreal and Ottawa.

Correia, J. I. E. et al. (1993) 'The Social Dimensions of Economic Structural Adjustment Programmes in Southern Africa — with special reference to Mozambique, Paper presented at the Winter School on 'The Social Implications of Economic Structural Adjustment Programmes in Southern Africa' organised by the University of Zimbabwe and the Zimbabwe Institute on Southern Africa, Harare, 4-23 June 1993.

Dalla Costa, Mariarosa and Dalla Costa, Giovanni (eds). (1995) *Paying the Price: Women and the Politics of International Economic Strategy*, London and New Jersey, Zed Books.

Elson, Diane (ed.). (1995 edition) *Male Bias in the Development Process*, Manchester and New York, Manchester University Press.

Elson, Diane. (1991) 'Gender and Adjustment in the 1990s: an Update on Evidence and Strategies', Background paper for Inter-Regional Meeting on Economic Distress, Structural Adjustment, and Women, June 13-14, Commonwealth Secretariat, London.

European Union. (1992) 'Declaration of the Council and of Representatives of Governments of Member States Meeting in the Council on Aspects of Development Cooperation Policy in the Run-up to 2000' (known as 'Horizon 2000'), Brussels.

European Union. (1995) 'Structural Adjustment', policy adopted by the Development Council of Ministers, June 1995.

Green, R. H. (1991) *The Struggle Against Absolute Poverty in Mozambique*, SDA Project, National Directorate of Planning, Republic of Mozambique.

Green, R. H. (undated) 'Poverty, Rehabilitation and Economic Transformation: the Case of Mozambique', unpublished paper.

Palmer, Ingrid. (1988) *Gender Issues in Structural Adjustment of sub-Saharan African Agriculture and Some Demographic Implications*, ILO World Employment Programme Research Working Paper, Geneva, ILO.

Sparr, Pamela (ed.). (1994) *Mortgaging Women's Lives: Feminist Critiques of Structural Adjustment*, London and New Jersey, Zed Books.

Woestman, Lois. (1994) *World Bank Adjustment and Gender Policies: Strangers in the Night, Fleeting Acquaintances or Best Friends?*, European Network on Debt and Development (EURODAD) and Network Women in Development Europe (WIDE).

World University Service. (1994) *Education in Mozambique: Addressing the Approaching Crisis*, London, WUS.

3. What Price Lives and Rights?

A 1996 World Bank report, *Global Economic Prospects and the Developing Countries*, does not give us grounds for hope. It argues that: 'Increased participation in international trade improves resource allocation, enhances efficiency by increasing competition amongst firms, and induces learning and technology transfer, thus facilitating growth.' Weak and slow integrators, such as most low-income countries in sub-Saharan Africa, are insufficiently open to trade and foreign direct investment. While conceding that countries experience transition costs in liberalising and integrating their economies, the World Bank believes that 'these costs tend to be overestimated' (*Financial Times*, May 8, 1996).

A more detailed look at the recent history of a few Southern countries illustrates well the costs of economic integration and the shortcomings of market-led economic growth as a development strategy. No country is like another: each is different in history, culture and natural resources. Each is different in the size of population and the levels of equality or inequality. Each country, too, has a different colonial inheritance and a particular place in the North's geo-political and commercial world view. The Philippines, Mozambique, Bangladesh, Zimbabwe and Nicaragua are each very different, yet all were advised by the international financial institutions to adopt the same economic recovery measures. All were, and are, encouraged to deregulate many aspects of the economy including labour relations, to liberalise trade and to privatise public services and state-owned enterprises.

The Philippines: Opening up the Economy

Through the Medium Term Development Plan (MTDP) and other initiatives, the Philippines government of President Ramos proposes to promote 'people empowerment', to 'improve the quality of life of all Filipinos' and reduce the percentage of people living in poverty to 30 per cent by the end of his term as president.

The cornerstone of the MTDP strategy is 'opening-up the economy' to the full and free operation of internal and external market forces. The strategy, when even by government estimates around 50 per cent of people live in poverty (NGO estimates are that the figure is as high as 70 per cent), when a small elite control most of the land, capital and other resources, and when, most importantly, no systematic plan exists to ensure the majority benefits from the economic changes, is guaranteed to increase rather than decrease the numbers of women, men and children living in poverty. The strategy does not address these fundamental inequalities.

In 1986 at the time of the overthrow of the Marcos regime, the Philippines had a huge external debt. Subsequent governments were determined to be model repayers and follow the IMF/World Bank line on economic recovery. In the early 1990s, President Ramos pronounced the country's debt crisis over. He was not alone in this perception. The country had moved from severe to moderate indebtedness. The region generally is dynamic in terms of economic growth, and the Philippines was attracting private financial flows which enabled it to service its debts (FDC, 1995). The debt remains very high.

The Philippines MTDP aims to reach its stated GNP growth targets of 10 per cent by attracting foreign investment, by export promotion, and continued foreign borrowing (Piglas-DIWA, 1993). It aims to increase foreign exports by 18.8 per cent and foreign investments by 25.9 per cent in the period 1993-98. Amongst other measures designed to attract foreign investment are some which bear directly on the wellbeing of millions of Filipino women and men. New laws allow foreign companies to lease public land for a maximum period of 99 years and procure as much as 65 per cent of newly privatised corporations, and enable foreign banks to operate in the Philippines. The Labour Code was amended to insert the provision that only 'gross' violation of the collective bargaining agreement constitutes unfair labour practice. Furthermore, the Secretary of Labour was given powers to prevent the occurrence of strikes through 'preventive mediation' in certain so-called vital industries, such as, food and drink, banks and telecommunications (Raquiza, 1995).

Although GNP rose to 5.1 per cent in 1994 and to 5.5 per cent by late April 1995, unemployment also rose from 9.5 per cent in 1994 to 11.9 per cent by April 1995 (Briones, 1995).

Production for Export

Export promotion is a key plank of the Philippines government's MTDP. The Philippines has had export processing zones (EPZs) since the 1970s. These special industrial enclaves were set up to attract foreign companies with pledges of ready-built factories, power, water, sewerage systems and roadways. Additional incentives included tax holidays, repatriation of profits, and a workforce untrammelled by trade unionism or any other form of labour regulation. According to a 1994 report, a total of around 61,000 Philippine workers are employed in EPZs and 75 per cent of these are women, mainly young women, working in textiles, garments, rubber products, electrical goods and electronics.

Tomasa Lopez Moreno cooking on her new fuel-saving oven. Use of these ovens is promoted by the Community Movement. San Lucas, Nicaragua.
(Jenny Matthews)

The Baguio City Export Processing Zone is a typical example. In September 1993, 12 years after its formal inauguration by President Marcos, 2,975 workers were employed in the zone, 2,079 or 69.88 per cent women. In total, 73 per cent of workers are in production and 27 per cent in management and staff positions; women comprise 83 per cent of production workers but only 33 per cent of management and staff. The government's expected level of 10,000-15,000 workers has never been reached (CWERC, 1994).

A number of unfair labour practices characterise work within the Baguio City zone and other zones in the Philippines and elsewhere; a ban on trade union organisation within the zone, non-observance of minimum wage levels, compulsory overtime, long hours, hazardous conditions, and insufficient health and safety precautions. Sexual harassment is also prevalent. But jobs are scarce and desperately sought after and, for the most part, jobs in the zones offer higher wages than are available outside. From their study of workers in another zone, the Mactan Export Processing Zone, Sylvia Chant and Cathy McIlwaine (1994: 25) found that foreign companies tend to be better at adhering to statutory regulations on wages and benefits and providing additional perks to workers such as private medical insurance. By contrast, Filipino companies, already disadvantaged in the global market, offer lower wages and worse conditions in the attempt to reduce costs and retain some competitiveness. A variety of mechanisms are used by companies to keep wages down, such as probationary schemes which mean that workers can be paid around 75 per cent of the minimum wage and may not receive full statutory social security for periods of up to six months.

Despite their management's anti-union stance, women workers in the zones have organised effectively to assert and defend their rights. The history of the zones is marked by frequent action over such issues as non-payment of wages, excessive work targets and withheld bonuses. Although workers often succeed in their strike or protest action, it is the employers who have the upper hand. At any point they can close the factory and remove the equipment in the full knowledge that jobs elsewhere are scarce and workers plentiful.

To attract foreign investment, the Philippines — in common with many other governments — openly advertise the 'docile nature' of their women citizens. A Philippines Department of Trade and Industry report talks of women's 'capacity for boredom' and states: 'passive and obedient, women can be made to work even straight through eight hours and pressured to meet high quotas often with minimum complaints' (Perpiñan, 1989: 83). Their unequal status in Philippines society, their family and social obligations, poverty and lack of employment opportunities undoubtedly combine to ensure that women, for the most part, endure long hours, routine work, unequal pay and harsh management. Gender-based inequality, reinforced by the prohibition of trade union organisation and official approval allows the companies to contain and exploit women. Women Working Worldwide writes (1991: 202):

They [the companies] have also received considerable support in this from: national governments which do not implement or enforce equal pay legislation or health and safety regulations; family expectations and social conventions which define precise roles for women; and men, who with their conflicting loyalties as co-workers, trade unionists, fathers, brothers and husbands, all too often oppose women and side with the "system".

Jobs in export processing zones enable women workers to earn income and develop an identity for themselves outside their home and family life. The income they earn is vital to the survival of their families. Making a significant contribution to household finances can enhance a woman's position in relation to her husband and family. With more money, some women workers can off-load some family responsibilities to others, usually other women, in return for pay or keep. In their study of Mactan EPZ, Chant and McIlwaine also found that young women gave a projected age at marriage of 25 years, which was higher than for women of that age group in the same area (Chant and McIlwaine, 1994). They attribute this delay to a desire on the part of the young women to save money for future studies or business ventures and also to diminished pressure to marry from parents who benefit greatly from the single woman's financial contributions to the household (normally 50 per cent of her salary). However, the long hours of employment and family responsibilities leave women little time for study or advancement, or for spending some of their earnings on personal pleasure.

While individual women zone workers may achieve change in their relations with men, this change does not immediately benefit all women. There is little evidence of overall changes in division of responsibilities between women and men. Filipino women zone workers still hold primary responsibility for family and household maintenance and survival. There is little change either in gender relations: there is scant evidence of men changing their attitudes towards women, assuming increased family responsibilities, or cutting down their recreational pursuits (Chant, 1996). In Chant's view, gender inequalities are reinforced through a combination of legal, cultural and social factors. Divorce is illegal in the Philippines. Women who set up house alone with their children are likely to be regarded with suspicion and as 'sexually available'.

Women are appointed to rigidly sex-segregated and labour-intensive occupations, as machinists, assembly-line workers, packers and clerical workers. The abilities women bring to this work are not recognised as real, and rewarded as such, but somehow as innate or natural to women. There is little scope for women workers to change to more highly skilled jobs within the factory or to be promoted to supervisory or managerial positions. Such stereotypical employment and lack of occupational mobility are unlikely to improve women's self-esteem or confidence. By contrast, men are appointed to jobs which require working with heavy machinery or heavy loads, and to supervisory (and sometimes to management) positions. Once they are mechanised jobs done by women frequently become jobs for men. It has to be said that occupational mobility for men is quite limited also; male factory floor workers are rarely promoted to management.

Large-scale open-cast mining causes deforestation, soil erosion, water and air pollution, and destroys the livelihoods of small-scale mining communities in the Cordillera, the Philippines. (Andy Rutherford/ One World Action)

The companies take full advantage of women workers' situation. The stereotype is that women are not the primary earners in their households, so they can be paid low wages. At the same time, the companies count on women's reliability, knowing that they cannot readily quit as their families' survival depends on their income. There is also a fundamental precariousness about employment in export processing zones. Global demand for products, economic upturns or downturns, company restructuring or enhanced profitability elsewhere all determine how long companies remain in any one location and thus affect the stability of women's employment.

The push for export-oriented production has explicit limitations as a long-term development strategy. The contribution to export revenue is important: the earnings from the four Philippines zones was US$666 million in 1992 (EIU, 1993). In most cases, the hoped-for technology transfer and spin-off stimulus to economic development outside the zones has not materialised and EPZs remain quite separate from the rest of the economy. The vast majority of the companies operating in EPZs are foreign-owned; a minority only have Filipino partners or subsidiaries. The number of jobs is low, little training is provided, and senior management positions are few and frequently held by non-nationals. Furthermore, the companies have little reason or commitment to stay in one location beyond the honeymoon period; many move to other countries in the region, such as Vietnam, where more attractive incentives are available. National development plans and priorities take second place to the interests of the transnational companies, which determine which products are produced where, for markets they control.

The push for export-oriented production has explicit limitations as a long-term development strategy.

The primary incentive for Japanese, US or European companies to relocate part or all of the production to a country like the Philippines is economic, not humanitarian or developmental. Relocation offers companies enormous savings in wages and overheads which offset any additional costs they may incur, for example, in transportation.

A recent phenomenon in the Philippines as elsewhere, South and North, is the rise in subcontracting and other forms of contractual arrangements. Large companies, foreign or domestic, subcontract out to smaller, usually domestic, companies which run small production units or contract home- or out-workers. The advantages of subcontracting for large transnationals and domestic companies are obvious: they strengthen market and technological control, reduce their overheads and avoid any nationalisation process that may take place. Well-known transnationals and domestic companies with reputations to maintain do not have to manage large factory workforces and can step aside from any allegations of exploitative labour practices. The employment conditions of contract and out-workers are marked by low wages, few or no benefits, and no job security. In addition, it is very difficult for contract and out-workers to organise to protect their rights. Subcontracting is becoming increasing popular throughout the industrial sector and throughout the global economy.

Increasing production for export is a basic tenet of the neo-liberal model of economic development. This strategy is not confined to the manufacturing sector; it dominates the entire Philippines economy. There has been a rapid increase in the activities of export-oriented transnational agribusiness. Vast tracts of the best land are being converted to growing so-called 'high-value' export crops such as bananas, pineapples, soya, cotton, asparagus or flowers. Similarly, in an effort to revive the ailing mining industry, the Philippines Government passed the Mining Act of 1995 (known as Republic Act 7942). This Act introduced incentives and removed restrictions on foreign investors making it easier for foreign (and local) mining companies to exploit vast tracts of mineral-rich land, much of which is the ancestral lands of indigenous peoples. Under this act, foreign investors would have 100 per cent control of large-scale mining operations and the right to repatriate all profits (IBON, 1996). The export of labour is yet another facet of the export-led strategy; the promotion of migration and its consequences are discussed in Chapter Four.

The emphasis on production for export multiplies the vulnerability of the Philippines economy to market forces beyond its control. The emphasis on production for export multiplies the vulnerability of the Philippines economy to market forces beyond its control. It intensifies the exposure of workers to the exploitation and the hazards of working in a deregulated labour market. The development of national industries is neglected, as are the needs and interests of millions of Filipinos, particularly women. As poverty and insecurity increases, the likelihood of creating effective domestic demand declines. The state, too, is weakened by this export-led strategy: tax-free holidays for foreign companies and repatriation of profits mean lost revenue. This in turn increases reliance on indirect regressive taxation, such as VAT, which hits the poor hardest.

Mozambique: Economic Rehabilitation?
(Research and documentation by Beverley Duckworth)

Mozambique was ripped apart by a vicious war of destabilisation, backed by the then South African regime, throughout the 1980s. Millions of women, men and children were displaced within the country and many more forced to flee to neighbouring countries. The political, economic and social life of the country was totally disrupted.

In 1984, Mozambique was in economic crisis and faced unserviceable debts. Several years of destabilisation and war since independence in 1975 had hampered all attempts to develop. The economy was in no position to absorb the effects of policy mistakes made in some sectors by the Frelimo government. From 1980 to 1986, Mozambique's GDP fell by 21 per cent (Africa Recovery, 1993). The manufacturing sector was in decline due to the war, shortage of inputs and its weak foundations resulting from the colonial period. UNICEF estimates that the destabilisation campaign cost Mozambique US$5.5 billion in physical damage and lost production in the period from 1980 to 1985. Agriculture, the most important sector of the economy, accounting for 80 per cent of the country's export earnings and employing 80 per cent of the workforce — 60 per cent of whom are women — was devastated by the war (Fleming, 1993). Millions of peasants, historically marginalised under colonialism, were forced to leave their land and take refuge in more secure areas or in neighbouring countries. Rural infrastructure and marketing were severely disrupted.

In 1984, Mozambique joined the IMF and the World Bank and began to liberalise its economy. The Economic Rehabilitation Programme (PRE) implemented between 1987 and 1990 was a standard structural adjustment programme. Yet, as a war-torn country, Mozambique was not like many other debt-burdened developing countries. It was in no position to argue a special case: a refusal to conform to the policy prescriptions of the international financial institutions would result inevitably in less aid and investment.

The international financial institutions failed to take account of the devastating effects of the war on Mozambique. They failed, too, to recognise Mozambique's colonial inheritance which had left it with few trained Mozambicans, inadequate government systems, a weak internal market and an economy geared towards serving the needs of the former colonial power.

The international financial institutions failed to take account of the devastating effects of the war on Mozambique.

Short-lived Economic Successes
The PRE did achieve initial economic successes. Between 1987 and 1989, export earnings rose rapidly, investment increased and the real GDP grew at an average of about 5 per cent each year. The per capita growth rate was smaller, at an average of 2 per cent, but this was nevertheless a significant improvement on previous years (Brochmann and Ofstad, 1990). However, these initial economic successes were unsustainable: the underlying problems of the economy were not addressed, and the economy was, and still is, heavily dependent on external assistance from the international donor community in the form of aid, spare parts and other industrial inputs and consumer goods. Given that a sizeable proportion of financial assistance comes in the form of loans rather than grants, Mozambique has accumulated a debt which in 1993 amounted to four times the country's GNP (Plank, 1993). Relative to the size of the formal economy, it is now one of the most heavily indebted countries in the world (Plank, 1993). Although implementation of the PRE has allowed the rescheduling of repayments on these loans in the short term, Mozambique is piling up future debt service liabilities which, according to even the most optimistic estimates of economic recovery, it will be unable to repay. Thus, its dependence on external financial assistance is not likely to disappear in the foreseeable future; it has become a permanent state of affairs.

Improving Agricultural Production

A major objective of the PRE reforms was to reverse the decline which had occurred in agricultural production and shift resources towards the rural population hardest hit by the war. The World Bank's policy focused on price incentives for rural producers, distribution of state land to the private and peasant sectors, and promotion of export production, as key aspects of agricultural reform (Gibbon et al., 1993). Few among the rural population appear to have benefited significantly from the policy reforms, while many have found their situation deteriorating. Although the effects of the war and the severe drought which hit Mozambique in the early 1990s were very significant factors, there were also serious flaws in the assumptions on which the PRE was based. The PRE failed to consider peasant farmers' low productive capacity or the state of rural infrastructure and marketing. The lack of transport and the closure of the state marketing board made the marketing of crops difficult for anyone living at any distance from the main marketing centres. Private operators were too few to fill the gap left by the state marketing boards. The particular situation of women farmers was either not understood or ignored.

Although the PRE sought to transfer resources towards small and private farmers, who have the highest productivity and efficiency levels, this was to be through price incentives rather than by direct investment support (Mosca, 1993). A 1988 evaluation of the first year of the PRE revealed that minimal resources were going to family farming, and thus to women farmers who represent over 90 per cent of family agricultural workers (Casimiro et al., 1991; CIDMAA/COCAMO, 1989). The price incentives approach proved ineffective as people's ability to respond to these incentives depended on the availability of resources such as land, credit facilities, information and training. The rural poor, and particularly rural women, usually have only limited access to these resources. Although price increases of up to 100 per cent were allowed for some crops, prices for main food items not produced by peasant households also rose sharply, as did agricultural inputs such as seed and fertiliser as a result of devaluation under the economic reforms (Marshall, 1992). In addition, the emergency food aid distributed at the same time as the PRE was underway depressed the prices for some agricultural goods (Mosca, 1993). So, after an initial improvement in 1987, the terms of trade for rural producers began to deteriorate again and became worse than before (Marshall, 1992; Hermele, 1990).

The PRE failed to channel the desperately needed investment into agriculture and particularly towards women farmers. The cuts imposed by the PRE on the Ministry of

The PRE failed to channel the desperately needed investment into agriculture and particularly towards women farmers.

Agriculture fell, and continue to fall, disproportionately on the recurrent budget. The level of spending was far too low to improve rural services and infrastructure in order that smaller farmers, who have to rely on traders for their produce sales, can benefit. In fact, the economic reforms meant that smaller producers entered into the liberalised market in a position of weakness, leading to the entrenchment of existing inequalities.

The Economic and Social Rehabilitation Programme (PRES) which followed the PRE in 1990 did place more emphasis on public expenditure in the family agricultural sector (Fleming, 1993), but most investment has continued to be concentrated on large-scale projects and in export agriculture dominated by medium and large companies (Hermele, 1990; Mosca, 1993). No attempt has been made to diversify production away from cashews and cotton, which are Mozambique's main export products. In 1992-93 alone, cotton prices fell by 44 per cent (World Bank, 1993).

The emphasis on agriculture for export also compounded the situation of food insecurity in rural areas. Cotton demands the most labour-intensive work at the same time that the majority of work is required for growing domestic food crops (Bowen, 1992); thus, increased pressure is put on women's time and labour. Land has been given over to production for export as opposed to domestic food production (Mosca, 1993). Also, a system of contractual farming emerged, whereby large agricultural companies use small farms to undertake some of their production. As a result, small farmers use less time and land for subsistence farming for local consumption and become locked into a dependence on the agricultural companies and their demands for particular crops, inputs and techniques (Melamed, 1993).

Accelerating Poverty

The World Bank food security survey of 1989 showed that rural food stocks were extremely fragile and inadequate, indicating the failure of the PRE to benefit the peasantry who had been so profoundly hit by the debilitating effects of the war (World Bank, 1989 in Bowen, 1992). Meanwhile, in the urban areas, which escaped the worst of the war, poverty has increased as a direct result of the policy reforms prescribed by the World Bank and the IMF. People now refer to the PRE as the 'PRI' — the individual recovery programme — for while a small number of Mozambicans are visibly prospering, namely middle to large traders, private entrepreneurs and cash crop farmers, the majority have been plunged into deeper cycles of poverty (Marshall, 1991).

Women-maintained households — 14.2 per cent of all households — have found it particularly difficult to cope in the harsh economic climate. Not only do women have fewer hours available to earn an income, because of family and domestic responsibilities, but the income they earn is extremely low; women in Mozambique earn three to five times less than men (Fleming, 1993). As one woman from Cabo Delgado commented: 'Before we stood in line to buy the few products that were available; today we queue just to look at all the things we cannot afford' (CIDMAA/COCAMA, 1989: 127). Today, the richest 20 per cent of the Mozambican population receive 70 per cent of the total cash income (Hermele, 1990). While this may not represent a dramatic departure from the situation before PRE, the poor, and particularly women, are finding it harder and harder to survive.

Today, the richest 20 per cent of the Mozambican population receive 70 per cent of the total cash income.

Mozambique is now one of the world's poorest countries. Who is responsible? Plank (1993) points out that the government of Mozambique cannot be held responsible as it has followed all the conditions laid down by the international financial institutions.

The impact of the Economic Rehabilitation Programme on agriculture in Mozambique is a stark illustration of the inappropriateness of unquestioningly applying text book economic theories to complex social, political and economic situations. With regard to Mozambique, as elsewhere, there appears to have been little analysis of the specific situation and needs of the country, let alone the specific needs and interests of Mozambican women farmers and how these could be met. The ability of small farmers, particularly women, to respond to the price incentives and switch to producing other crops was severely restricted by their limited access to land, credit, information and training. Once again, macro-economic preoccupations have dominated policy-makers' thinking; they did not focus on the poverty of the majority of people living in the rural areas and thus the poor become poorer.

Bangladesh: Stabilising and Adjusting Poverty?

In Bangladesh, the number of women, men and children living in absolute poverty has increased every year since independence. Agriculture is the primary economic activity but the vast majority of those who live in the rural areas have no land. A relentless process of landlessness and impoverishment has occurred over the past two decades as those with some land borrowed to buy essential seeds and fertilizers, became indebted and lost their land. The periodic river floods, and periodic cyclones in the coastal areas, have pushed more and more people into poverty.

In the late 1970s, like many countries, Bangladesh faced external and internal deficits and was left with little option but to approach the IMF and World Bank. In return for loans, Bangladesh agreed to undertake a stabilisation and structural adjustment programme. Stabilisation policies were introduced in the late 1970s and early 1980s but a full-scale structural adjustment programme was not installed until 1991. The key elements of the economic plan include: liberalisation of tariff barriers and import bans, privatisation or denationalisation of state-owned enterprises (SOEs), and the promotion of production for export.

Bangladesh has been heavily dependent on aid since independence. Now, around 70 per cent of Bangladesh's development budget is funded by external aid and loans (it had previously been higher).

Garments for Export

Bangladesh is different from the Philippines in almost every respect, yet it too is pinning many hopes on production for export. In the years from the late 1970s to the early 1990s, the Bangladesh garments industry expanded dramatically from a few factories to around 1,630 factories by late 1993. Proceeds from the export of ready-made garments reached US$1.2 billion in 1993 and constituted 52 per cent of total exports compared with 1.1 per cent in 1981/82. The net export value, when imported input costs are subtracted, was US$420 million in 1993. The industry is now Bangladesh's biggest exporter.

High unemployment and poverty mean that Bangladesh has many women and men looking for waged work, and willing to work for relatively low wages. This is the single most important factor in the growth of the garment industry. The industry requires little investment in equipment, complicated technology or expensive factory space. Most firms are small or medium sized and run on foreign finance; 80 per cent are based in the capital, Dhaka, and most others in Chittagong. They cut and make garments for around 250 international subcontractors, and all fabrics, designs and specifications are supplied by the buyers. The garments industry employs around 800,000 workers, 84 per cent of whom are women or young girls, and a significant number of whom are the primary or only source of income within their households. The industry is not without its hazards: long hours, low health and safety standards, for example, coupled with limitations on organising.

A number of factors led large numbers of young women to seek employment outside the confines of the home. These included growing poverty and landlessness, and migration from rural to urban areas, widening access on the part of girls to some education within the context of a secular state. The growth of the garment industry is inextricably linked to the increasing participation of women in the urban industrial labour force. As is clear from the Philippines and elsewhere, manufacturing industries like to employ young women who are perceived to be submissive, willing to work for low pay, have little experience in trade union organisation, and are easily dismissed when market fluctuations necessitate retrenchment or relocation.

With all these qualifications, and in the context of growing poverty, landlessness and institutionalised gender inequality, the garment industry provides much needed and much coveted job opportunities to thousands of women. The industry, with all its vulnerabilities to the whims of the global fashion market and protectionism, cannot offer sustainable livelihoods to the millions of Bangladeshi women and men seeking employment.

Farming Shrimps

In the coastal areas of Bangladesh it is estimated that around 30 per cent of women from rural areas have some involvement with small-scale fishing, including coastal fishing and freshwater aquaculture. In addition to the more traditional work of making and repairing nets and processing and storing fish, women are increasingly involved in inland freshwater fish farming. Farming shrimps for export is a growing business in Bangladesh, as in other countries in South-East Asia. Shrimp farming, like garment making, is tied closely to meeting the demands of Northern consumers.

The World Bank, in particular, played a key role in promoting intensive prawn farming as a useful foreign currency earner. At a first glance, farming shrimps seems economically sensible: Bangladesh has a wealth of rivers and deltas, and it is possible to produce up to four 'crops' per year, and prawns are nutritious.

Prawn farming does create some new employment, particularly for women, building embankments around the prawn ponds, maintaining the service roads and weeding the shrimps fields (Christian Aid, 1996). Although wages are low, the income they provide is critical to the women, but the work is seasonal and widely regarded as menial and bestowing little esteem. Prawn farming also provides short-term employment opportunities for men in construction of roads and buildings; children, too, are involved and can earn money by collecting prawn fry.

On closer examination, intensive prawn farming can be seen to be both environmentally and economically unsustainable. Freshwater wells in villages and fields become contaminated by the salt water from prawn ponds, and the removal of trees and embankments make villages more vulnerable to cyclones. The traditional method of rotating rice cultivation and wild fish farming on alternate seasons was sustainable. Now, rice fields are ruined.

The prawn industry has been accompanied by unrest and violence. Demonstrations by local people against the expansion of the prawn industry into their fertile rice fields and good pastures frequently end in violence as hired thugs attack the protesters. In 1991, one woman, Karunamaye Sardar, was killed and several others were injured. Her death is commemorated locally each year. It is a constant reminder of how the needs and interests of local women and their families are ignored.

Intensive prawn farming has turned out to be a quick fix providing good short-term profits to the prawn industry. The industry offers little or nothing in the way of long-term economic security and, in fact, has damaged the traditional farming and fishing livelihoods. A more sustainable approach to economic development in rural Bangladesh would emphasise small-scale prawn production, protection of agricultural land and much more local involvement and control.

Deepo Pandar Shudeer, senior paramedic of Gonoshasthaya Kendra (People's Health Centre) in Savar, Bangladesh. GK runs a village-level health care programme which combines primary health care, education and training.
(Jenny Matthews)

Privatising State-owned Enterprises
Following independence in 1971 the new Bangladesh government took ownership of all property, factories and banks abandoned by their previous Pakistani owners. From that date, it began a gradual process of denationalisation. By 1994, the public sector was still large, including, for exam-

ple, commercial banks, insurance companies and a range of industries from paper, fertiliser, sugar, to steel and ship yards. In the early 1990s, the Bangladesh government stepped up its programme of denationalisation.

Undoubtedly many state-owned enterprises (SOEs) were poorly managed, overstaffed and loss-making. According to World Bank figures, the losses of all SOEs, including railways, in the fiscal year 1993 were equivalent to 27 per cent of the budget of the Annual Development Programme, 45 per cent of external project aid, and 2 per cent of gross domestic product. As these losses were financed from state-owned commercial banks, they affected the whole financial system and indirectly other industries. The World Bank's remedy was 'rapid progressive privatisation' of selected SOEs, initially in manufacturing; secondly, those SOEs which would remain in public hands were to be 'pushed to commercialise and face the market'; and thirdly, private sector involvement was to be facilitated in key utilities (such as power, gas, water) and key infrastructure (such as telecommunications and transport) to increase efficiency. The programme of privatisation planned was simultaneously too ambitious, too drastic and too rapid.

Invest in EPZs in Bangladesh.
Advert

The privatisation of the jute industry illustrates the problems. Jute is a major cash crop for around 3 million small farming households. It is the largest industry, producing one-third of manufacturing output, earning 20 per cent of total export revenue, and providing 10 per cent of all employment and 12 per cent of GDP. In 1993, there were 64 jute mills in operation, 30 of which were fully publicly owned. Following a World Bank evaluation of the jute industry in 1992, a plan was drawn up to close down 18 jute mills, laying off 25,000-30,000 workers, almost all of whom are men, and to sell most of the rest to private investors. A variety of means were used to shed workers, ranging from straightforward dismissal to forced resignations and voluntary redundancy.

Garment factory workers protest the three month long non-payment of their wages. Dhaka, Bangladesh. (Ron Gilling/Panos Pictures)

Golden handshakes and training were to be offered to assist retrenched workers and their families to find alternative means of earning a living but most workers did not even receive the three-months severance pay to which the 1965 labour law entitled them. A survey of 75 workers carried out in 1994 by Ain O Shaish Kendra, a legal aid organisation, threw up some interesting results. Eighty per cent of the workers interviewed received between 15 days and one month's pay although the official records stated that three months' pay had been granted. Such compensation as was received was sharply reduced in value due to corruption or delayed payments. Most workers had to wait seven to eight months to receive their pension, gratuity and other benefits and had to pay substantial amounts in bribes to officials and trade union leaders to receive what was due to them. Similarly, the promised programmes of retraining did not materialise. None of the workers surveyed received the promised golden handshake.

The retrenchment of thousands of jute workers has had repercussions throughout Bangladesh and pushed not only their immediate families into further poverty but also many others in related industries and services. Ahmed (1995) estimates that around one-quarter of Bangladesh's people is involved in some way with the jute industry, either directly or in related activities in agriculture, marketing, manufacturing or trade. There was no analysis of the implications the reorganisation of the jute industry would have for Bangladeshi women or for gender relations.

There is little evidence that sufficient numbers of Bangladeshi entrepreneurs or foreign companies will emerge to deliver the scale of production for export that the country needs to meet its economic growth targets or provide employment for the jobless and landless millions of women and men. Some SOEs had to be withdrawn from the market due to lack of private sector interest. At present, foreign investors, or domestic investors, do not find Bangladesh sufficiently attractive.

...an economic reform programme which increases unemployment in the short term and which promises few new jobs seems particularly inappropriate.

In a country with high levels of poverty and very low levels of employment within the formal sector, an economic reform programme which increases unemployment in the short term and which promises few new jobs, seems particularly inappropriate. Bangladesh experienced 5 per cent growth in the early 1990s but the cost of this growth has been high. Atiur Rahman, of the Bangladesh Institute of Development Studies, asks if the growth rate and the basis of the growth are good enough to eradicate extreme poverty by the end of this century. He writes (1994):

> Can we really sustain even this moderate growth rate? Is this growth broad based so that even the very poor can participate in the activities which generate this? Apparently, the present growth processes are not yet poverty reducing. Rather in many cases they augment poverty by enhancing income inequality and wastages of natural resources endangering environment and the welfare of our future generations.

The phenomenon of jobless growth is not unique to Bangladesh. The policies of production for export and privatisation of state-owned enterprises are part of the neo-liberal economic reform package designed to achieve fiscal stability and economic recovery. But once again, the concentration on macro-economic considerations has obstructed any clear thinking on how to reduce the poverty, economic vulnerability and marginalisation of most Bangladeshi women, men and children.

Nicaragua: Privatising Health Care
(Research and documentation by CEAL, Centro de Estudios y Analysis Socio Laborales)

Throughout the 1980s, Nicaragua suffered a crippling war of destabilisation waged by the Contras and backed by the United States against the Sandinista government. The war put enormous strains on the economy, diverting 50 per cent of government revenue into defence and away from economic reconstruction and social development. Throughout the 1980s, Nicaragua was starved of much-needed foreign assistance by the US, the UK and the World Bank. This aid and loan boycott was overtly and undeniably ideological.

In 1990, the Nicaraguan people elected a new government formed by the United National Opposition (UNO), a coalition of 14 small parties. The people were tired of the war, tired of economic hardship, and they voted for peace and an end to the blockade. They hoped a new government would attract aid and investment and bring economic recovery. Their hopes were not fulfilled. It quickly became apparent that voting out the Sandinistas was not in itself sufficient to appease the donors and investors. Nicaragua now receives more aid than during the 1980s, but with strings attached; aid is conditional on implementing a harsh economic reform programme. The Nicaraguan government embarked on its stabilisation and structural adjustment programme in 1991. Public spending on the national health service was to be one casualty.

In 1982, the World Health Organisation praised Nicaragua for its progressive health care system set up by the Sandinista regime. It was a system which placed great emphasis on primary health care, carried out mainly through the work of thousands of health promoters and brigadistas (brigade workers) in the cities, towns and rural areas. Their role was to work with local women and men in their communities to improve health through education, the use of low-cost techniques such as immunisation and oral rehydration, and water and sanitation improvements. The inoculation of children under one year rose from around 20 to 80 per cent during the 1980s. People's Health Councils were established to involve communities in planning, implementing and evaluating health care. As in the classic primary health care model, conditions which could not be handled at the local health unit were referred to district or regional hospitals. The success of the health system was reflected in falling infant and child mortality rates and in a drop in the number of women dying in childbirth or from pregnancy-related causes.

Boiler plant workers in pharmaceutical factory set up by Gonoshasthaya Kendra (People's Health Centre) to produce essential medicines at affordable prices.
(Jenny Matthews)

The UNO government set about dismantling the national health system. The reform programme included the privatisation of the Ministry of Health (MINSA), a reduction in health personnel, privatisation of pharmaceuticals, restoration of the pre-1980s employment-related private medical services linked to social security, and the curtailing of trade unions. The UNO government was thwarted almost immediately in its reform plans: a conflict arose between the reform programme of the Ministry of Finance and MINSA which produced its own Master Health Plan in 1991, giving priority to infant and maternal services, control of epidemics and the decentralisation of services. The conflict is still evident today but reforms go ahead. Aid agreed in 1991 for MINSA from the official US Agency for International Development (USAID) and loans from the World Bank and the Inter-American Development Bank were held up pending introduction of the reform programme.

Health Cuts

Between 1987 and 1989 the Sandinista government spent an average of US$35 per capita on health. By 1994, expenditure on health had fallen to US$16 per head, a 60 per cent cut. A Pan-American Health Organisation study estimates that in constant 1988 US dollars, spending on public health went from an average of 100 million in the years 1984-87, despite the war, to 72 million in 1992 (Evans, 1994). This reduction in public spending immediately led to massive cut-backs in the number of health workers. The job conversion programme launched in April 1991 alone made 2,959 health workers redundant — medical staff and general workers such as cooks, cleaners and porters (Evans, 1994). The Health Ministry froze the programme in August 1991 but continues to suffer from a high turnover of staff due to low pay and demoralisation.

To conform with the conditions of Nicaragua's Extended Structural Adjustment Facility signed in April 1994, the government put increasing numbers of health workers on temporary contracts. The aim is to end all collective agreements, create a flexible labour force, and clear the way for easy dismissals. Since the beginning of 1994, the Ministry of Health offers only temporary contracts to health workers.

Health sector training was also hit badly. Between 1993 and 1994, the government concentrated on reducing their contractual obligations to health sector trainees. Medical interns were awarded grants in place of government contracts. The period of training for social service trainees was reduced from two years to one. At the same time the number of trainee technicians was cut.

The net result is large numbers of unemployed health workers. Health specialists have not been immune to the health reform programme: there was a 50 per cent reduction in the three years from 1990.

As part of the reform package, a programme of user fees for health services was introduced with the encouragement of USAID and the World Bank. The professed objective was to introduce to the Nicaraguan people the concept of paying for health. In most places people now pay a fee of 5–10 cordobas (US$0.85–1.70) to see a doctor. It is officially estimated that only 30 million cordobas can be raised through health charges, that is less than 5 per cent of the health budget.

The quantity and range of medicines available in Nicaragua were also affected by the health reforms. Accord-

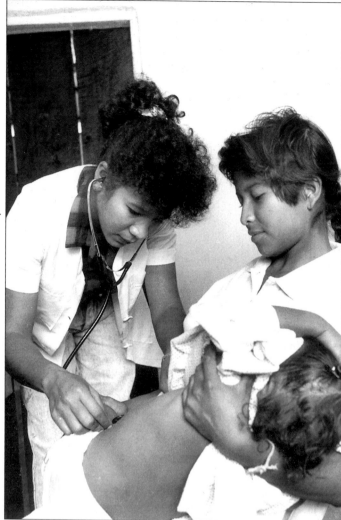

*The privatisation of
health care in
Nicaragua has led to
women making fewer
visits to health posts.*
(Jenny Matthews)

ing to the Pan-American Health Organisation study, spending on medicine dropped sharply from a high of US$28.3 million per year in 1980–83, to US$7.2 million a year in 1989–92 (Evans, 1994). Controls on the importation of pharmaceuticals were lifted in 1990, opening the way for uncontrolled importation and price rises. The practice of centralised buying was abandoned. The government body, COFARMA, which had imported, regulated and distributed medicines for the Ministry of Health went into liquidation in 1991 due to lack of funds and credit. COFARMA had served to control the price of drugs in the private sector by selling direct through community pharmacies. With COFARMA gone, the private sector can charge what it pleases. Commercial labels have also been reintroduced undermining the previous essential and generic drugs policy. The Ministry of Health continues to have a role in managing those drugs prioritised within the limitations of the health budget. A new body, the Centro Insumo para la Salud, is in charge of buying and selling drugs on the open market.

In 1994 the Institute for Social Security and Welfare (INSBII) took steps to set up separate health care structures for the small minority of workers in formal sector employment (estimated at 5 per cent) who pay social security. INSBII will buy services from the Ministry of Health which has agreed to provide hospital care, including emergency and intensive care, but not treatment for chronic illnesses, in the publicly funded hospitals in Managua. FETSALUD, the largest health sector union, regards these developments as the first steps towards privatising health care, establishing a two-tier health system and subsidising health services for better-off workers and their families at the expense of the public sector (CEAL, 1994).

Impact on Health

A deterioration in quality and quantity of services was quickly evident in some areas, with increases in the incidence of low birth weight, infant deaths and deaths of women from pregnancy- or childbirth-related causes. These are linked mainly to malnutrition, insufficient provision and quality of ante- and post-natal care, user fees and lack of institutional medical care for those in need. Pregnancy and childbirth have become more dangerous for many women. To save money women, with a low income may decide not to seek ante-natal assistance but these are the very women most likely to have complicated births due to overwork and undernourishment.

One undeniable, yet inevitable, result of the health reforms will be to exacerbate existing gross inequalities in access to health care and perpetuate the vicious cycle of poverty, malnutrition, low birth weight and ill health. The Pan-American Health Organisation study showed that people have reduced the number of visits they make to the doctor. There is also evidence that people are turning to alternative medicine; one estimate puts this as high as 73 per cent. While this may a positive development, it indicates that huge numbers can no longer afford conventional health care. Amongst the most common health problems in Nicaragua are those respiratory illnesses which are usually chronic. Young children are particularly affected when coughs or colds develop into bronchitis. Just as common are the illnesses related to diarrhoea and, in the rainy season, malaria. These illnesses are preventable and treatable. But as

Migdalia Hernandez, a young health worker with eight years' experience, recounts:

> When a child falls ill its mother usually goes to the Health Centre where the doctor gives her a prescription. When, as often happens, the health centres are right out of medicines, the only recourse is to buy them from a private chemist's shop where the minimum cost of a cough syrup is 10 cordobas (US$1.70). Of course, this means that the woman cannot buy the medicines because most of them are just too poor and what little money they get hold of has to go on food (One World Action, 1994).

Hospital pharmacy, Matagalpa, Nicaragua. The health service reforms have led to reduced spending on medicines while at the same time the costs of medicines have risen.
(Jenny Matthews)

Accurate data on the levels of malnutrition does not exist but the widely-held view is that malnutrition is increasing, particularly in the poorest areas of the country; this would account for the outbreaks of measles and scabies. The Ministry of Health's own figures place infant mortality at 81 per 1,000 live births, but it is as high as 197 in some areas. Sixty per cent of infants are anaemic and 35 per cent of children under five years are malnourished. Seventy-four per cent of households earn less than 1,000 cordobas per month which is the estimated cost of the basic basket of goods per month. In a 1994 report, the Food and Agriculture Organisation estimated that 68 per cent of Nicaraguans were suffering from acute calorie deficiency. Other serious health problems include HIV and TB but, in Nicaragua, few resources for education and treatment are available.

Wider Implications

The privatisation of health care has implications beyond health and wellbeing. The practice which developed during the 1980s of popular participation and worker debate on issues of public health has little scope for operation in the new Nicaragua. FETSALUD, which represents 16,000 out of 20,000 health workers, has taken an active part in resisting the health reforms in the period since 1990 and its representatives have defended the health budget in the National Assembly. The union has participated in all stages of the health reform talks with the Ministry of Health. It organised two national strikes in February/March 1992 and November 1992/January 1993 to protest against proposed changes. It successfully negotiated a new collective agreement in December 1993 for two years. In August 1993, FETSALUD convened a national assembly of 1,000 trade unionists to discuss and prepare a document on the 'Basic conditions for reforms and principles for national health policies'.

Sixty per cent of infants are anaemic and 35 per cent of children under five years are malnourished.

FETSALUD's active participation in protecting the Nicaraguan health service has not received widespread approval from the donor community. In Nicaraguan government agreements with USAID and the World Bank, the opposition of trade unions is mentioned as a risk factor in the implementation of health service reforms. In April 1994, the newspaper *Barricada* accused the government of promising the multilateral donors it would veto the proposed new labour law and introduce policies which would 'promote flexibility'.

The three-year Extended Structural Adjustment Facility agreement signed with the IMF in the spring of 1994 required a further 4.9 per cent cut in public sector spending, improved cost recovery for education and health services, and a continued credit squeeze for small and medium producers. During his visit to Nicaragua in April 1994, Michel Camdessus, President of the IMF, is alleged to have said: 'The poor are going to have to suffer' (*Barricada*, April 8, 1994).

The Nicaraguan government has serious problems fulfilling its agreements with the IMF and failed to meet key targets in its economic stabilisation programme for the period March – September 1995. In early 1996, it was under enormous pressure from the IMF to comply with a revised plan which included a commitment to undertake partial privatisation of BANADES, the Nicaraguan Development Bank. BANADES was under pressure to close 53 offices and lay off 800 bank workers. In order to repay its debts to the Nicaraguan Central Bank, BANADES suspended all credit for the agricultural season. BANADES was one of the few remaining sources of credit for small- and medium-scale

Regulating Pharmaceuticals (Bangladesh)

With its National Drugs Policy 1982 (NDP 1982), Bangladesh sought to reform the nation's pharmaceuticals market with the intention of providing cheap and effective medicines for all, curbing the use of harmful and useless drugs and countering irrational use of drugs. This was in line with the policy of the World Health Assembly which in 1982 urged member states to adopt essential drug lists, generic names, tougher drug legislation, strategies for reduction of prices and a code of drug marketing practice. The NDP 1982 enacted all the recommendations of the World Health Assembly. (World Health Assembly, 1992)

The Policy met with some very serious opposition from the numerous parties connected with the drug industry in Bangladesh. This opposition found a new and powerful ally in the shape of the World Bank which on April 13, 1992 'recommended', *inter alia*, that new products be allowed to be introduced by using free sales certificates; all price controls be lifted; and the control of drug advertising be removed from the drug licensing authority. This was at a time when developed countries were starting to impose regulations on pricing and advertising.

Seventy per cent of the world's people live in Southern countries and yet consume only 14 per cent of the world's total supply of medicines. Although per capita expenditure on drugs is high in such countries as Japan (US$400) and Germany (US$215), the sum spent is only 8–10 per cent of the total health expenditure for the nation. In the South, where the sums spent on drugs vary from US$2 to US$15 per capita, it represents from 22 to over 60 per cent of total health expenditure, meaning fewer funds for other areas of health spending. This skewing of health expenditure is made worse by the promotion of irrational drug use in poorer countries, where poorly developed regulatory apparatuses and quality control mechanisms have led to an excess of large numbers of brand-named drugs and a surfeit of conventional and other medicines of highly doubtful efficacy. The consequence of the promotion and prescription of irrational drugs is that a large number of unnecessary, useless and even harmful formulations are allowed onto the market. Many of the drugs on the U.N. Consolidated List of banned, harmful and restricted drugs are freely available in a large number of Southern countries and this problem is compounded by many factors. Besides poor regulation and quality control, there is high consumer illiteracy, coupled with unethical practices by pharmaceutical companies and a medical profession often unaware of the politics and marketing strategies of the companies and the economics of drug production and health care.

The NDP of Bangladesh went a long way towards tackling these problems and was widely praised by the World Health Organisation and UNICEF. Now, however, the World Bank's promotion of liberalisation and deregulation in every sphere of the economy is undermining the government's NDP. The result of this is that while these ground-breaking medical reforms still exist largely in the spirit in which they were created, the opposition has made significant encroachments on the NDP and it could well become a pale and ineffectual shadow of its former self. (Source: Chowdury, 1995 and Endicott, 1995)

farmers. Most rice and beans eaten by Nicaraguans are culti-
vated in the first growing season which starts in April. The
lack of credit, coupled with the already precarious financial
situation of most farmers, seriously jeopardised the success
of the 1996 farming season.

*Andrez Miranda, with
new pump installed
by the Community
Movement as part of
their programme of
community development.
Madriz, Nicaragua.
(Jenny Matthews)*

Is This People-centred Development?
Surely it cannot be beneficial to the long-term economic
development of Nicaragua to deprive millions of women,
men and children of basic wellbeing and health care. Even
if ideology and commitment to the concept of mutual solidarity are put aside, it seems cavalier and invidious to introduce drastic health reforms at a time of dire economic crisis,
when 75 per cent of households are registered below the

poverty level, without taking adequate steps to protect the health of the poorest people. The loss of employment in the health care service, coupled with the loss of essential services and rising costs of care and medicines, have a direct impact on womens' lives. Women have had to turn to precarious and exploitative sectors to earn some income, while more and more precious and hard-to-earn income goes on health needs rather than food and other daily essentials. Women's own health is also put in jeopardy as the costs of services such as ante-natal care can become unaffordable.

Nicaragua in the 1980s was notable for the positive measures it took to promote and protect women's rights and advance gender equality — measures in health care, education and training, employment and child care. This infrastructure of gender equality is now dismantled.

The post-war opportunity for long-term equitable development has been lost and the economic crisis is deeper now than it was in the 1980s. Nicaragua has the largest per capita debt in the world and debt servicing takes more than 60 per cent of GNP. The country's trade deficit grew from US$292 million in 1992 to US$582 million in 1993. Nicaragua's problems have been augmented: as well as suffering from indebtedness, devastated public services and a ruined economic base, it has lost its previous position of strength within the Central American region; furthermore, Nicaraguan women's full enjoyment of their equality and human rights has been postponed.

Zimbabwe: Positive Action in Jeopardy

Women cannot compete with men on an equal footing in either the formal or informal sectors in any country worldwide. Differentials in basic rights, education and skill training levels, and access to resources such as land, combined with the burden of family and domestic responsibilities and discriminatory attitudes, place women in a prejudicial position vis à vis men. In the formal sector, women face problems of getting and keeping jobs and being trained and promoted. When employment is found, they usually face additional discrimination: lower wages, less promotion and sexual harassment. The gap in earnings between women and men remains a constant and obstinate barrier to women's equality. Low wages weaken women's position in the labour market and maintain their dependence on men; this in turn becomes the rationale for women's ongoing responsibility for housework, thus freeing men for better and more secure jobs. However, this is changing: unemployment among men is increasing as lower wages make women the preferred workforce in export manufacturing, for example. (The trend in the North is that most new jobs are part-time and for women.)

While entry into paid employment does not on its own guarantee equality in gender relations, it is an important step in that direction. For women who are isolated and invisible in the marginal informal economy, paid employment in the formal sector can offer visibility and social, economic and political power.

In order to redress the bias against women in employment, many countries have embarked on recruitment and training programmes designed specifically to ensure that employment and promotion opportunities are open to women. Such positive action programmes require the political will of governments and commercial enterprises and their commitment to allocate time and financial resources. This commitment becomes considerably weaker in times of economic hardship. The case of Zimbabwe is illuminating.

ESAP in Zimbabwe: No Time for Equality

The Economic Structural Adjustment Programme (ESAP) on which the Zimbabwe government embarked in 1990 contained a commitment to reduce the public service workforce by 25 per cent (25,000 workers) by 1995. This was in addition to the usual neo-liberal economic reform measures to liberalise trade, specifically to allow a greater range of imports, both raw materials and manufactured goods, and measures to deregulate investment and labour conditions. Each measure was guaranteed directly or indirectly to increase unemployment and decrease domestic demand. From the beginning of the ESAP in 1991 to the fourth quarter of 1994, 20,710 workers had lost their jobs, mostly in mining, engineering, transport and agriculture. The Zimbabwe Congress of Trade Unions believes the total· figure to be as high as 30,000 and to include around 13,000 public sector workers. The impact on household income has been harsh: real income levels in early 1995 were lower than at independence in 1980 (*Financial Times*, January 26, 1995). By late 1994, over 1 million women and men were unemployed, up from 400,000 in 1987 (EIU, 1994:15).

In the years following independence, the Zimbabwean government took some measures to promote equal rights and equal opportunities for women at various levels of society. A Department of Women's Affairs was established in 1981. Various pieces of legislation were passed during 1980 on, for example, minimum wages, equal pay for equal work and maternity leave. A legal age of majority act was passed in 1982, giving African women majority status (previously in Zimbabwe, African women of all ages were treated as minors under the law). The Labour Relations Act of 1985 prohibited discrimination in employment on grounds including sex. Changes in labour legislation were matched by action in the area of primary, secondary and tertiary education. In 1980, the government introduced a policy of free primary education which was particularly beneficial to girls. By 1990, enrolment rates for girls and boys in primary schools had increased rapidly with little difference between the sexes. At secondary and tertiary level, the ratio between the sexes remained heavily skewed towards males. The reintroduction of primary school fees at the end of 1991 appears to be jeopardising the progress already made towards educational equality.

Literacy classes are vital to women's empowerment, Bangladesh. (Jenny Matthews)

An Example of Positive Action

An interesting positive action policy was introduced in 1990 by the Public Service Commission in Zimbabwe to accelerate the advancement of women into management positions. The policy stated that there would be 'positive discrimination' in promotions to middle and senior management positions in favour of women until a target figure of 30 per cent women was reached (this was the percentage of women at the entry levels). It was planned to reach the target within two years of implementation of the programme. A number of measures were initiated in February 1991 to put the policy into practice. Ministries were requested to nominate women for promotion (274 women were nominated), vacancies were notified to ministries, nominated women were included among interview candidates (even if they had not applied). A similar request was made to all ministries to nominate candidates for management training, resulting in a list of 125 women. Appropriate training was organised or identified by the Manpower Planning Unit which in turn set a target of 30 per cent for all its scholarship and training programmes. International donors, like the British Council and the Canadian and Swedish international development agencies assisted with funding.

The positive action programme did not meet its target in two years (Chari, 1993). Around 20 per cent (56) of the 274 women nominated for promotion achieved promotion; two women reached Deputy Secretary level and 11 Under-Secretary level. Progress was also slow on the training side. Yet progress has been made. Chari identified a number of factors which hindered the success of the programme: lack of clear and adequate information about the policy, consequent resistance and resentment by some males, fear and lack of confidence on the part of women themselves. Other factors included the lack of a consistent position with respect to briefing the beneficiaries, attitudes in society, women's social responsibilities, and complacency and lack of motivation by some women. Lack of additional personnel and special administrative structures to look after the programme and lack of proper sensitisation training for male managers of the programme, were additional problems.

Chari writes that the Public Service Commission is still committed to the programme and says it will continue although she acknowledges that its implementation is slowed down due to the ESAP. She is sceptical about whether in the grave economic environment it is possible to maintain, let alone increase, the momentum. Furthermore, pressure to reduce the civil service will continue, she argues, and job insecurity and increased competition for fewer jobs may increase male hostility to the programme.

Equality for women within employment, as the above example demonstrates, requires high level political commitment, a substantial reallocation of resources, systematic public education, and a stable economic environment. The rigours of the Economic Structural Adjustment Programme in Zimbabwe, as in the case of economic reform programmes elsewhere, demand that the labour market, as well as finance and commodity markets, are allowed to operate freely without restraint or regulation. But the labour market does not inherently operate without bias as unequal gender relations mean that women do not compete equally with men. This inequality is exacerbated in times of economic austerity. The necessities of gender equality require positive action to eliminate structural biases in the marketplace.

Equality for women within employment requires high level political commitment, a substantial reallocation of resources, systematic public education, and a stable economic environment.

Unresolved Issues

Even a passing glance at the situations of Nicaragua, Mozambique and Bangladesh would indicate that none of these countries could withstand the rigours of the classic IMF/World Bank stabilisation and structural adjustment programmes. The recommendation to stabilise, produce for export and grow presuppose a moderately well-developed agricultural and industrial base able to compete in world markets. But even in the Philippines and Zimbabwe, which in many respects are stronger than Nicaragua, Mozambique or Bangladesh, the economic reform programmes have brought increased social and economic destruction. The poverty level in each country is so great, as in many countries in Latin America, the Caribbean, Africa and Asia, that investment in health care, education and employment creation, and the strengthening of mechanisms to ensure better distribution of wealth and resources, would appear a more reasonable strategy for long-term and equitable development, rather than sharp reductions in public spending across the board and a free rein for the small elite who control land, capital and other resources. The approach of the international financial institutions and the donor community to these countries represents the triumph of dogma and text-book macro-economics over common sense, justice and humanity.

What About Land?

There are some critical holes in the dogma. The whole issue of land use and ownership is one. While the international donor community makes many rhetorical gestures towards land reform, effective land redistribution does not figure prominently on its agenda and is never given priority in practice. It would appear that time and time again, the international donor community is unwilling to upset powerful vested interests and its stated commitment to enhancing the productive capacity of the poor does not stretch to ensuring that the poor have the resources with which they could be productive. Southern governments are equally disinclined to dismantle the current inequitable land ownership structure or to surrender their own privilege.

...its stated commitment to enhancing the productive capacity of the poor does not stretch to ensuring that the poor have the resources with which they could be productive.

The Philippines demonstrates the problem. There, as in many countries, land is key to survival for millions of people and critical to social and economic justice. Only 15 per cent of the 10 million Filipino agricultural workers own the land they work on. Since 1986, when Cory Aquino came to power, many thousands of acres of agricultural land have been converted for use as industrial, commercial, residential or tourist belts. Thousands of peasant farming families, who

*Young girls and boys
are active members
of village reforestation
work in Somoto,
Nicaragua*
Jenny Matthews

depend on rice production for survival, are being displaced
onto more marginal land such as hill sides, where farming
is difficult, or are forced to migrate to crowded urban or
coastal areas, or abroad. Land use conversion is helped by
the derailing of the Comprehensive Agrarian Reform
Programme (CARP) initiated in 1988 which aimed to redis-
tribute 10.3 million hectares of land over a period of 10 years.
As of 1992, 363,276.65 hectares of agricultural land had been
distributed under Emancipation Patents but of this women
control and own less than 9.9 per cent. Women did not fare
any better under the Certificate of Land Ownership Agreements. By 1992, only 18 per cent of the beneficiaries were
women. In both cases, not only did fewer women benefit but

also on average women received less land per head than men. There are no statistics to indicate how women-maintained households (14 per cent overall in the Philippines) benefited from the agrarian reform programme. In general, the indication is that even within the limited land redistribution carried out, the male prerogative of owning and inheriting agricultural land has remained intact despite legislative changes to recognise women's rights to economic assets.

The process of acquiring Emancipation Patents and Certificates of Land Ownership is not without its hurdles and costs. Peasant women and men had to borrow considerable sums to purchase certificates and those unable to meet the annual repayment sums were frequently forced to relinquish the title. In 1994, the National Federation of Peasant Women (AMIHAN) reported that many of its members had become badly indebted in order to acquire land under CARP. Land speculation also put much land outside the reach of small peasant farmers. In addition, legal loopholes allowed large land owners to retain their estates. Estimates are that less than 7 per cent of land was distributed.

'How could a nation supposed to be on the road to NIC-hood wake up one day without rice to feed its people?'

The Philippines experienced a rice crisis in mid-1995 when rice shortages reached serious levels. The crisis highlighted the fundamental flaws in the agricultural and development policy which gives priority to land conversion to tourism and mining and production for export at the expense of growing food for local consumption. The *Manila Times*, in December 1995, summed up the contradictions: 'How could a nation supposed to be on the road to NIC-hood wake up one day without rice to feed its people?'

In Mozambique, too, access to and ownership of land are critical to survival. As elsewhere, it is women who are losing out in the struggle for land. Since 1987, in Mozambique, it has been legal to enter into leasehold arrangements, and a market in land has been established. Land is becoming a source of speculation, a reserve of riches for the future. Small producers are being dislodged in the areas around the towns, in the irrigated valleys and along the main transport routes. The growing unemployment and impoverishment caused by the economic reform programme (PRE) have led to increased pressure on land as more families turn to growing crops to sell and eat. The war and the displacement of millions of peasants have increased competition. This competition has occurred in the context of the distribution of state land by the government. Although some of this land has been passed to vulnerable groups, the emphasis on large-scale production and access to capital in deciding distribution has meant that foreign and large private companies have benefited disproportionately (Melamed, 1993).

Since the introduction of the PRE, the agricultural cooperatives around Maputo, 95 per cent of whose 8,500
members are women, have had to fight off attempts made
by private farmers to take over their land (Bowen, 1992).
Many women have been forced to hire lawyers in order to
secure their rights to the land. The issue of women's land
rights is fraught with problems, not the least of which is the
disparity between customary or traditional laws and
modern civil codes. President Celina Cossa of the Union of
Cooperatives of the Maputo Green Zone has been at the
centre of these struggles:

> Peace is when we cease to be murdered with bayonets and
> firearms because we support Frelimo and our govern-
> ment. Peace is also not being thrown off our land by
> bandits who, though they do not carry machine guns, are
> armed with the cannons of opportunism with which they
> want to restore exploitation (Hermele, 1990: 24).

She has also expressed concern that the growing emphasis on privatisation in Mozambican agriculture has devalued
the status of the country's farming cooperatives:

> They say that with the PRE, what is important is private
> initiative. But there are many ways of developing private
> initiative. As poor people, we feel the need to unite
> together and work in co-ops (Marshall, 1991: 7).

At a meeting in 1990 to discuss access to and ownership
of land, one woman voiced her concerns plainly:

> Big foreign companies may be able to produce much more
> than the peasants. But then what will become of us? The
> companies set their machines to work, and they don't
> even need our labour. And they will produce for export,
> not to feed the people (Bowen, 1992: 26).

This need has been particularly strong in the poorer
Northern regions, where cooperative membership has now
become a survival strategy for small farmers, and especially
women, to increase their access to services and security to
land (Melamed, 1993: 51). These cooperatives are now faced
with a lack of resources as the growing number of peasants
joining have little else but their labour to contribute.

Land is a highly controversial issue in Zimbabwe, too.
Following independence in 1980, the government of
Zimbabwe promised to implement a programme of land
reform. Little progress has been made. A comment from the
Economic Intelligence Unit in their report for the third quar-
ter of 1994 sums up the situation well:

The lack of planning and the derisory allocation of land redistribution in the recent budget demonstrates yet again that there is no intention to implement the sort of radical land reform that would promote greater social equality... Some land may be transferred; however it will not be land from inefficient white farmers (of whom there are many) to thousands of landless peasants, but rather from random, eccentric or politically insensitive whites to already well-off blacks (EIU, 1994: 4).

Without land and the resources, especially credit, and freedom to farm it effectively, women, and all small farmers in developing countries, cannot benefit from the incentives offered by the economic reform programmes. Women, in particular, have very restricted land rights, and their access to technology, training, credit and farming inputs is similarly limited. Ensuring women's rights to land through inheritance or purchase is a critical first step towards food security and economic well-being for the poorest women and their families. Economic policy, whether conceived externally or internally, if it is to create sustainable development, must concern itself with ensuring that the poor, and particularly women, have access to and control over resources.

Export-led Development?

The reliance on production for export also raises as many development questions as it purports to answer. It is hard to understand the heavy emphasis on production for export within the IMF and World Bank economic thinking. Evidence from the 1960s and 1970s indicates considerable asymmetry between value of export production to the companies involved and value to the general economy in terms of sustainable development. A policy of production for export which fostered the development of local companies could bring longer-term economic advantages. However, local companies for the most part cannot compete on the global market. The reality indicates that the promotion by the international institutions and donors of export-led development, when coupled with the 'free market' and deregulation, has more to do with the expansionary objectives of international capital and transnational corporations and less, if anything, to do with the long-term sustainable economic development of the countries such as the Philippines.

Although there is some evidence that the pace of industrial relocation from the North to the South is slowing down due to automation, unemployment-related cheaper labour in the North and trading block restrictions (NAFTA; EU), new export-processing zones are being planned in South-

East Asia and elsewhere, and existing zones are being expanded.

For countries like Nicaragua, Bangladesh and Mozambique, among the very poorest countries in the world, it is hard to see how they can attract sufficient foreign investment to build essential services and infrastructure, create employment and significantly reduce poverty. The costs of attracting investment are high. Take the example of Mozambique. In order to attract investment into a country so disrupted by war, Mozambique had to offer substantial incentives, such as the waiving of import duties and the offer of large tax concessions. Mozambique has one of Africa's most flexible policies on repatriation of earnings, allowing some investors to export from the country up to 80 per cent of hard currency profits and resulting in money flowing out of the country almost as fast as it comes in (CIDMAA/COCAMO, 1989: 126): As Melissa Wells, US Ambassador, commented, Mozambique is 'dismantling the machinery of central economic control' and 'there's almost nothing they're not prepared to do to get investment' (CIDMAA/COCAMO, 1989: 125). Mozambican capitalists complain of preference being given to foreign investors. For instance, even before a new national policy had been created to open up investment in tourism, local traders and hoteliers found that foreign companies had already secured the best opportunities (Bowen, 1992). Mozambican industries are still heavily dependent on imports which have increased in price due to currency devaluation. They are not strong enough to compete with the industries of neighbouring countries (Bowen, 1992). The smaller and informal sector enterprises complain that they do not have the resources to take advantage of the credit and input support which has been established for medium and small scale enterprises (Green, 1991).

The type of investments that have been made by foreign investors, have not been conducive to developing the productive capacities of the Mozambican economy. Investment has been concentrated in sectors serving the regional economy, in agro-industry and in large, capital-intensive projects which make little use of local resources and capacities (Hermele, 1990). Bowen (1992: 25) contends that the PRE is facilitating the establishment of 'a weak, dependent form of capitalism which basically will serve the South African economy with labour, transport routes, markets and raw materials without contributing to sustainable development, a picture just like the colonial era'.

The costs are high in other ways too. Southern governments have to extol the virtues of their workers in the international labour market. Asian governments vie with each other to sell the 'nimble fingers' and obedience of their women workers to prospective foreign investors and happily remove or set aside all protective labour laws.

Central to the economic strategy followed by countries, such as Bangladesh, Nicaragua and the Philippines, and to the model promoted by the international financial institutions and donor governments, is labour flexibility. Their rationale is as follows. Access to productive jobs with fair remuneration is the only way out of grinding poverty for the poorest. To encourage private investment and employment creation, inflexible wage-bargaining agreements, poor labour-management relations, and misguided labour regulations must be changed. Centralised systems of setting wages, links between public and private sector wage agreements, and a national minimum wage are regarded as undue interference and a disincentive to investors. Governments must remove themselves from the labour market and allow maximum flexibility.

Life or Debt – women oppose IMF/World Bank Structural Adjustment policies. Center For Women's Resources, the Philippines

The World Bank and others acknowledge that other measures will have to be taken to strengthen 'desirable' labour institutions and appropriate safeguards for workers to ensure their rights under national and international standards are not violated. In its 1995 World Development Report the World Bank conceded that trade unions did have some role in economic affairs (World Bank, 1995). It is undeniable that labour markets could benefit from some transformation. Rigidities which protect the interests of privileged skilled or high-paid workers can do little to advance the cause of those who are low-skilled and low-waged. The World Bank and others also concede that to expand access to productive jobs, especially those with more sophisticated production processes, workers must have access to appropriate education and training. However, many structural adjustment programmes are leading to cuts in education and training, and so the contradictions continue.

The attitude which the international financial institutions and the international community have towards workers' organisations can also be seen in their response to people's organisations. In Nicaragua, Bangladesh, Mozambique, Zimbabwe and the Philippines, women's organisations, community-based organisations and NGOs are strong and vociferous about the impact of neo-liberal economics and the growing social, economic and political marginalisation of millions of people. They have organised protests, strikes and demonstrations. They have insisted that their voices and views be heard and acted upon. They have pressed for alternative policy priorities and presented alternative policy options. In the Philippines, for example, the Freedom from Debt Coalition, together with a large alliance of peoples' organisations, trade unions and others, campaigned successfully about the hike in the price of oil and again about increases in VAT. In Bangladesh, community organisations, researchers and NGOs have highlighted the devastation caused by aggressive economic reforms. In Nicaragua, FETSALUD, the largest health workers' union, has been unstinting in its resistance to the privatisation of the national health care service. Other unions have fought against the privatisation of the national telecommunications company. Trade unions and women's organisations have also taken the lead in resisting the economic reforms in Zimbabwe and Mozambique. The official response to such displays of opposition has varied from place to place and from time to time, ranging from violent repression, to total disregard, to dialogue.

And the 'Gender Gap' Grows
There is little evidence that neo-liberal economic reform programmes have created the conditions for equitable gender relations and sustainable economic development in any country.

The World Bank's analysis, as outlined in its 1994 policy paper, of why women face barriers in contributing to and benefiting from development is interesting:

> The barriers begin with comparatively low investment in female education and health, they continue with restricted access to services and assets, and they are made worse by legal and regulatory constraints on women's opportunities (World Bank, 1994: 7).

The World Bank then identifies five areas in which, it argues, 'evidence of what works is particularly strong': education, health, wage labour, agriculture and natural resource management, and financial services. It is difficult to match this analysis with the evidence of countless Southern organisations, research institutions, international and national NGOs, and some intergovernmental organisations that women's access to education, training, health services, employment, land and credit has sharply declined, from an already low point, in the last decade or so — a decade which coincides with the World Bank's own pre-eminence in shaping economic choices in most Southern countries.

The World Bank's concern at the 'gender gap' is widely shared by the international donor community but this concern is not mirrored in mainstream policy or practice. It is undeniable that investment in female education and health care has been, and is, grossly inadequate in most Southern countries, but what is also true is that such progress as was made in, for example, Nicaragua, Zimbabwe and Mozambique in the 1980s, is now stalled or in reverse. The increases in poverty, inequality and marginalisation in the countries discussed in this chapter demonstrate that policy-makers need to look beyond rates of growth in GNP, balance of payments numbers, inflation rates and money supply and to adopt gender-sensitive indicators and analysis which show what is happening at the meso- and micro-levels of economic activity.

policy-makers need to look beyond rates of growth in GNP, balance of payments numbers, inflation rates and money supply.

World Bank and IMF-style economic reform programmes, which are backed with some important qualifications by most bilateral donors and the European Union, are exacerbating the underlying causes of women's inequality and doing nothing to adjust the political, economic and social structures which discriminate against women at every level and perpetuate gender-based inequality. In fact, they depend on that inequality. Sustainable economic and social development cannot be created as long as the inequality between women and men persists.

Chapter Four looks at the responses from the international community to the evidence of social and economic dislocation resulting from the economic reform process. It looks, too, at how millions of women, men and children are responding and coping with the ramifications of the economic reforms.

References

Africa Recovery. (1993) *Mozambique: Out of the Ruins of War*, Briefing Paper No. 8, May, New York, UN Department of Public Information.

Ahmed, Nilufar. (1995) 'Debt Crisis, Structural Adjustment Policies and Impact on Workers in Bangladesh', Dhaka, Ain O Shaish Kendra.

Ain O Shaish Kendra. (1994) 'Survey of the Adamjee Jute Mills' quoted in Nilufar Ahmed. (1995) 'Debt Crisis, Structural Adjustment Policies and Impact on Workers in Bangladesh', Dhaka, Ain O Shaish Kendra.

AMIHAN (National Federation of Peasant Women). (1992) 'Their Failure Become Our Strength', conference proceedings from Asian Peasant Women Dialogue on the General Agreement on Tariffs and Trade and Structural Adjustment Programs, Las Britas Hotel, Antipolo, Rizal, Philippines, 9-18 November 1992.

Barricada, April 8, 1994, Managua, Nicaragua

Bowen, M L. (1992) 'Beyond Reform: Adjustment and Political Power in Contemporary Mozambique', in *The Journal of Modern African Studies*, No. 30, Vol. 2, Cambridge University Press.

Briones, Leonor Magtolis. (1995) 'The Philippines: Higher Growth, Fewer Jobs', unpublished paper for Freedom from Debt Coalition quoted in Report of the Philippines Alliance for the 52nd Session of the UN Commission on Human Rights March 18-April 26, 1996

Brochmann, G. and Ofstad A. (1990) *Mozambique: Norwegian Assistance in a Context of Crisis*, Bergen, Chr. Michelsen Institute.

Casimiro, Isabel, Laforte, Ana and Pessoa, Ana. (1991) *A Mulher em Moçambique*, Maputo, Centro de Estudos Africanos.

CEAL (Centro de Estudios y Analysis Socio Laborales). (1994) *Nicaragua's Health Service Reforms 1990-1994*, London, One World Action.

Chant, Sylvia and McIlwaine, Cathy. (1994) 'Gender and Export Manufacturing in the Philippines: Continuity or Change in Female Employment? The Case of the Mactan

Export Processing Zone', paper prepared for Gender Issues Panel, European Conference on Philippine Studies, School of Oriental and African Studies, University of London, April 13-15 1994.

Chant, Sylvia. (forthcoming 1996) 'Women's Roles in Recession and Economic Restructuring in Mexico and Philippines' in Alan Gilbert (ed.). (1996) *Poverty and Global Adjustment: the urban experience,* Oxford, Blackwell.

Chari, Unity A. (1993) *Positive Action Measures to Promote the Equality of Women in Employment in Zimbabwe,* Working paper from ILO Equality for Women in Employment Project, Geneva, ILO.

CIDMAA (Centre d'Information et de Documentation sur le Mozambique et l'Afrique Australe)/COCAMO (Cooperation Canada Mozambique). (1989) *Mozambique 1989 — New Directions,* Canada.

Christian Aid. (1996) *After the Prawn Rush: the Human and Environmental Costs of Commercial Prawn Farming,* London, Christian Aid.

Chowdhury, Zafrullah. (1995) *The Politics of Essential Drugs: the Makings of a Successful Health Strategy, Lessons from Bangladesh,* London and New Jersey, Zed Books.

CWERC (Cordillera Women's Education and Resource Center) and WWP (Women Workers Program). (1994) *Women Workers Situation at the Baguio City Export Processing Zone,* Baguio City, CWERC and WWP

Economist Intelligence Unit. (1994) Zimbabwe Country Report, No.4, Zimbabwe. London, EIU.
Economist Intelligence Unit. (1993) Zimbabwe Country Report No. 1, London, EIU.

Economist Intelligent Unit. (1993) Philippines Country Report No. 1, London, EIU.

Endicott, David (1995) Bangladesh Drugs Policy: A Step Backwards?, *Briefing Paper,* London, One World Action.

Evans, Trevor. (1994) *The Impact of Structural Adjustment Programmes in the Public Sector in Nicaragua,* Managua, CRIES (Coordinadora Regional de Investigaciones Economicas y Sociales).

Fleming, Sue and Barnes, Colin. (1992) *Poverty Options in Mozambique: Strategy Options for the Future of UK Aid*, London, Overseas Development Administration.

Fleming, Sue. (1993) 'Women on the Side-lines: Policy-making and Poverty in Mozambique', paper prepared for the African Studies Association Meeting on Gender and Adjustment in Africa.

Freedom from Debt Coalition. (1995) *Strategy 1996-1998*, FDC, Manila

Garfield, Richard and Williams, Glen. (1989) *Health and Revolution: The Nicaraguan Experience*, Oxford, Oxfam

Gibbon, P., Havnevik K. J., and Hermele K. (1993) *A Blighted Harvest: The World Bank and African Agriculture in the 1980s*, London, James Currey.

Green, Reginald H. (1991) *The Struggle Against Absolute Poverty in Mozambique*, SDA Project, National Directorate of Planning, Republic of Mozambique, Maputo.

Green, Reginald H. (undated) 'Poverty, Rehabilitation and Economic Transformation: the Case of Mozambique', unpublished paper.

Hermele, K. (1990) *Mozambican Crossroads: Economics and Politics in the Era of Adjustment*, Bergen, Chr. Michelsen Institute.

IBON. (1996) *Hunger From Food Security*, Special Release, People's Policy and Advocacy Studies, Manila, IBON.

IBON. (1996) *Mining Act: National Patrimony Megasale*, Special Release, People's Policy and Advocacy Studies, Manila, IBON.

Marshall, Judith M. (1991) 'Resisting Adjustment in Mozambique: the Grassroots Speak Up' in *Southern Africa Report*, July

Marshall, J. M. (1992) War, *Debt and Structural Adjustment in Mozambique*, Canada, The North-South Institute.

Melamed, Claire. (1993) 'Structural Adjustment and Land Policy in Mozambique: the Creation of Structural Poverty?', unpublished MA Dissertation, University of London.

Miller, M. (1993) 'Mozambique's Crisis of Governance: a Look at Population Displacement, Societal Change and Post-war State Capacity', unpublished M.Phil Dissertation, University of Cambridge.

Mosca, Joao. (1993) *Alguns Aspectos Sobre os Efectos do PRE na Agricultura*, Estudos Moçambicanos 13, Maputo, Centre for African Studies.

One World Action, (1994) Joan Smith interview with Migdalia Hernandez, Uniles, Somoto, Nicaragua, April 11, 1994.

Pan-American Health Organisation (PAHO). (1993) *Condicions de Salud en las Américas: Nicaragua*, quoted in Trevor Evans. (1994)

Piglas-DIWA. (1993) 'The Ramos Administration Medium Term Development Plan (Philippines 2000): Prospects for Filipino Women',Newsletter of Center of Women's Resources, Vol. VI, No, 2, Manila.

Perpiñan, Sister Mary Soledad. (1995) *The Philippine Country Report on Women, 1986 - 1995*, Manila, Third World Movement Against the Exploitation of Women.

Plank, D. N. (1993) 'Aid, Debt and the End of Sovereignty: Mozambique and its Donors', in *Journal of Modern African Studies*, Vol. 31, No. 3, pp. 407 - 430, Cambridge University Press.

Rahman, Atiur. (1994) 'The Sting in the Tail of the Structural Adjustment Policies', Bangladesh Institute of Development Studies.

Raquiza, Maria Victoria R. (1995) 'Women, Debt, Free Trade and the Paradox of Development in The Philippines' *Briefing Paper*, London, One World Action.

UNICEF. (1987), *Children on the Frontline: the Impact of Apartheid, Destabilisation, and Warfare on Children in Southern and South Africa*, New York, UNICEF.

Women Working Worldwide. (1991) *Common Interests: Women Organising in Global Electronics*, London, Women Working Worldwide.

World Bank. (1995) *World Development Report, 1995* , Oxford and New York, Oxford University Press.

World Bank, (1994) *Enhancing Women's Participation in Economic Development*, Washington, World Bank.

World Bank. (1993) 'From Emergency to Sustainable Development', Paper for Consultative Group Meeting, Paris, December 1993.

World Health Assembly, (1982) *Resolutions WHA 31/32.*, Geneva, WHO.

4. Life on the Margins

When neo-liberal economic policies were adopted and implemented in the UK, in the US and later elsewhere, the social, economic and political reality was different in some vital respects from that of an indebted developing country. The UK, for example, has a relatively well-developed economic infrastructure and agriculture, industrial and service sector base and relatively high employment. It also has the capacity through favourable trade agreements to protect its commercial interests. It has a well-developed social infrastructure, national health and education systems, and a national social security system to provide protection to those in need. It has a long tradition of political opposition, free media and a diverse and vibrant civil society. Even so, the impact of neo-liberal economics in the UK has been high unemployment, increased poverty and growing gaps between rich and poor.

By way of explanation or excuse for the detrimental social and economic effects of the economic reform programmes, it is argued that many people in the South were just too poor to benefit from the reforms. The reality is that in most indebted developing countries, it is the majority, and not a minority, who are poor. To imply that somehow, inadvertently, the interests of the poor were missed in the design of structural adjustment programmes is a serious admission of incompetence, not to mention inhumanity. The model of economic reform adopted in the North was indiscriminately imposed on or promoted in the South. The reforms did not bypass the poorest, they struck them with precision: essential services were removed, living costs rose, and unemployment increased.

This chapter looks at three responses to the economic reform process. The first is the official welfarist response on the part of the international donor community in the form of safety net programmes designed to mitigate, in the short term, the detrimental social effects of adjustment and provide some assistance to those affected by rising unemployment and poverty. The policy-makers were convinced that only temporary assistance was necessary to assist 'the most vulnerable' through the transition period of the economic reforms. The second response comes from people — women and men who, further marginalised from the mainstream economy by the economic reform process, joined the informal sector as street traders, waste paper collectors and so on. The third response is migration. Women and men from the Philippines and other Southern countries leave home to work abroad as domestics or construction workers, for example. Migration is not solely a personal economic choice, it is an explicit policy of governments; for a country like the Philippines 'labour export' is a vital source of hard currency. Each response reflects the contradictions at the heart of the neo-liberal model of economic development.

Theatre group performance on the use and management of the new water supply. Sambiganza Project, Luanda, Angola.
(Bob van der Winden)

Safety Nets?
(Research and documentation on Nicaragua by Judy Butler and on Mozambique by Bridget M. Walker and Gabriel L. Dava)

In response to widespread evidence from UNICEF, Southern and Northern NGOs and others that structural adjustment programmes were further impoverishing the poor in the poorest Southern countries, the international donors led by the World Bank initiated a series of special social programmes. These safety net programmes took different forms in different countries.

In November 1987, the World Bank launched its Social Dimensions of Adjustment programme (SDA) specifically for sub-Saharan African countries. This was funded by the United Nations Development Programme (UNDP), the African Development Bank and other multilateral and bilateral agencies. The World Bank (1993) described the SDA as 'a strategic reaction to the nascent concern for the poor in the process of adjustment'. The programme was to reduce poverty 'for vulnerable groups' through specific actions but within the context of structural adjustment. The total expenditure on the SDA programme up to April 1992 was US$253 million, of which 63 per cent came from donors other than the World Bank.

The assessment report (World Bank, 1993) is enlightening. The authors admit that the SDA programme '... lacked clarity as to whether its purpose was to deal with the structural adjustment-afflicted poor, with poverty in general, or with the social dimensions of development'. One concluding sentence with regard to lessons for the future is even more illuminating: 'The enormity of Africa's poverty problems needs to be addressed on a much broader policy front. Under conditions of such pervasive poverty, it is also neither realistic not practicable to distinguish between the structurally poor and the conjuncturally poor once economic reform measures continue over many years.' The assessment report leaves the reader in no doubt that the World Bank and its brother donors got it wrong. In 1992, the SDA programme was brought to an end at World Bank level. But the free-market economic thinking continues.

The Social Dimensions of Adjustment programme in Mozambique provides a useful illustration of the strengths and weaknesses of the overall World Bank initiative and, although now finished, illustrates some issues concerning the donors' approaches to poverty (Walker and Dava, 1994).

In an attempt to counter the worst social and economic effects of the Economic Rehabilitation Programme (PRE) on certain groups within Mozambican society, a social component was added to the structural adjustment programme in 1990. The PRE thus became the Programme of Social and Economic Rehabilitation (PRES). The groups to be protected, so-called vulnerable groups, were women, children, people with disabilities, the elderly and displaced people — a sizeable percentage of the total population. The PRES adopted three additional strategies: the promotion of the use of labour intensive techniques; the rehabilitation of education and health systems to allow increased productivity and improvement of access to potable water to reduce disease; measures to improve household food security.

The SDA initiative was designed by a World Bank team based on the results of two 14-18 day missions to Mozambique in mid-1989 as well as discussions at the annual Paris Consultative Group meeting with the Mozambican government and donors later that year. In addition to World Bank staff, these missions included representatives from donor governments, including the European Community and the British Overseas Development Administration

(ODA). Meetings were held with key Mozambican ministries, research institutions and some international NGOs.

The SDA programme was managed by the World Bank in Washington and funded by four bilateral donors: the Dutch, Swiss, German and British governments. Each funded separate programmes of work and had different criteria and methods of working. The British ODA funded the policy development component, imposing certain conditions regarding the selection of advisers and participation in monitoring missions.

At the other side of the world in Nicaragua, a different form of safety net programme was initiated. Soon after President Violeta Chamorro took office in April 1990, her government began to restructure and redefine the guidelines of ministries such as health, education and social welfare, and other government institutions responsible for aspects of social policy. Within the first year it also set up three new social programmes under the Ministry of the Presidency, one of which was the Emergency Social Investment Fund (FISE). FISE bears many of the hallmarks of the World Bank's SDA programme, and many of its shortcomings (Butler, 1994).

The US Agency for International Development (USAID) was the main international agency active in setting up FISE and providing initial funding. The World Bank and Inter-American Development Bank (IDB) were consulted. FISE began in November 1990 but did not reach full operational capacity until 1994. At the end of 1994, FISE had 112 employees, 62 of whom were engineers, promoters and other specialists and professionals. FISE has succeeded in generating increased support each year. In 1994/95, its funds were US$138.41 million excluding another US$9.6 million in counterpart funds guaranteed by the government of Nicaragua. The IDB, USAID and the World Bank are the largest donors, contributing between them almost 80 per cent of total funds to date. USAID began phasing out its support in 1992.

FISE has eight stated objectives. These include: to strengthen actions to help alleviate poverty and generate temporary employment; to provide or rehabilitate basic services, giving priority to primary health care, basic education, and drinking water and sewage systems in marginal urban and rural areas. It also aims to strengthen community and NGO participation in the execution of projects and to develop the capacity of municipal governments and NGOs to administer and absorb resources at a local level. It plans to give special attention to the Autonomous Atlantic Regions and to contribute to the reactivation and development of the private sector.

Targeting 'Vulnerable Groups'
Both the SDA programme in Mozambique and FISE in Nicaragua aimed to alleviate poverty. Both programmes were inherently short-term and not designed to tackle the structural causes of poverty.

The Mozambique SDA programme consisted of two elements: the Policy Analysis and Data Programme (PADP) and the Social Action Preparation Programme (SAPP). The PADP was intended to strengthen the analytical and planning capacity of the government to develop policy measures on food security and the poor's access to basic services and participation in economic recovery. The SAPP was to assist the government in the development and evaluation of social action programmes and policies in order to increase employment and labour productivity, and improve urban food security and 'equitable access' to basic services. A Social Action Fund was set up to initiate pilot projects 'to improve vulnerable groups' capacity to participate in national economic development', with the further aim of improving policy formulation. Projects were to be small-scale and to operate in the areas of education, health, water, income generation, local infrastructure, and food for work programmes. They were to be based on community needs as expressed through local government or NGOs. Vulnerable groups included: severely malnourished children, people in rural areas lacking access to basic services, homeless young people in urban areas, the physically disabled, the young unemployed, women in the informal sector, and urban and peri-urban low-income families and the unemployed.

FISE is a financing arm of the Nicaraguan state for targeting the poorer sections of society. Its main activity is to obtain and administer external and domestic financing for the construction, reconstruction or repair of small-scale social and socio-economic infrastructure works and provision of social services. It promotes the submission of projects, evaluates their viability and appropriateness, contracts out those approved — when appropriate — to reliable private contractors, monitors their execution and concerns itself with ongoing maintenance. It also helps train central and municipal government authorities in diagnostic skills, identification of priority needs and project formulation. FISE requires that 30 per cent of any proposal budget go to labour. From an initial focus on accessible urban areas FISE expanded to include remote rural areas, particularly targeting zones designated as being in extreme poverty.

Forty-four per cent of FISE's project portfolio, as at late 1995, were small-scale projects to repair or construct schools; another 30 per cent were health related covering health posts, drinking water and sewage systems; the remaining 26 per cent included other social categories, environmental projects, and rehabilitation of roads, rainwater drainage systems, markets and slaughterhouses. FISE's activities in the Atlantic Coast, particularly the North Atlantic Autonomous Region, were very different: in addition to repairing schools, FISE focused on rural-oriented projects including road and bridge repair and maintenance, and reforestation activities.

Gender Optional

The intensely gendered nature of poverty was largely ignored both by the SDA programme in Mozambique and by the FISE in Nicaragua: there is no evidence that the particular situation of women was understood or that specific measures were adopted to tackle women's poverty. Gender-disaggregated data were not collected or used in the formulation of either programme.

Gender differentials were not included as a specific issue in the SDA programme design in Mozambique. Although women, for example in the informal sector, were named as a 'vulnerable group', almost the only time women were mentioned in the project document was as beneficiaries of the water standpipes project. Consideration of gender-related issues was left to the professional orientation and initiative of individual advisers. Similarly, the design of FISE contained little gender analysis, and there was no clear policy on how to address gender-related issues. Neither initiative analysed the gender implications of the structural adjustment programmes.

Poor Results

Even on their own terms — as short-term safety-nets — both programmes failed to make a significant contribution to the well-being of the poorest women, men or children. The direct impact of the SDA programme on the poor in Mozambique was minimal. It was widely regarded as attempting to 'paper over the cracks' in the design of the PRES which should have been subject to a more fundamental modification. Furthermore, it brought too little, too late; the worst years of the war and the initial years of the structural adjustment programme, when the need was greatest, preceded the SDA programme. No analysis was done of how the poorest women and men were surviving or how their survival strategies could be supported.

No analysis was done of how the poorest women and men were surviving or how their survival strategies could be supported.

FISE's role in poverty reduction was slight. Temporary employment on scattered small-scale construction projects cannot hope to make a serious impact in a country with 60 per cent unemployment, especially when no measures were taken to ensure that local workers, or those most in need, were hired. In addition, FISE's conditions — for example, that a contractor must be bonded for 15 per cent of the project value and this bond must be posted in Managua — made it unlikely that out-of-work builders in distant municipalities could effectively compete for contracts. The perception and/or reality that contractors do not hire labour locally is the biggest point of popular controversy about FISE. Construction unions complain that contractors cut workers' pay rather than their own profits in order to win bids.

The findings of an opinion survey of families living near a FISE project allow us to compare women's views with those of men (Renzi et al, 1994). Thirty six per cent of the women and 28.6 of the men interviewed believed that families in their community benefited from the FISE project through indirect employment, even though only 4.6 per cent of all households interviewed claimed to have received any indirect benefits themselves. In terms of direct employment, a family member had been employed in only 3.9 per cent of the households (4.7 per cent in female-headed ones and 3 per cent in male-headed ones). Only 2.8 per cent of the female-headed households believed that the project was directed at them.

Street trading in Duncan Village, East London, South Africa.
(Jenny Matthews)

FISE had no significant impact on malnutrition levels or on people's capacity to feed themselves. The programme made no attempt, for example, to provide the means for sustainable small-scale farming. Food security is now one of the biggest problems facing Nicaragua. The squeeze on credit resulting from the economic reform programme has exacerbated this situation.

Some Positive Outcomes

It would be misleading to imply that the safety net programmes in Mozambique and Nicaragua achieved nothing. In Mozambique, a new Poverty Alleviation Unit grew out of the SDA programme which reviews and coordinates poverty and food security policy. The SDA also made a contribution towards a system for poverty definition, analysis and policy-making which it is hoped will assist in the coordination of government and other agencies' responses to poverty. It also strengthened government planning capacity and supported staff training.

FISE did provide some access to basic social services for some of the poorest sectors of the population. The fact that FISE has taken over the investment role of ministries like health and education is a mixed blessing. In the short term, it allows those ministries to focus their energies on health and education provision, but in the longer-term, beyond FISE, it may result in a gap in social investment structures. It is positive that some of FISE's funding is earmarked for the institutional development of these line ministries, and that they are required to coordinate with FISE and guarantee the equipment and personnel for any construction in their area. While some institutions at government level were strengthened, this was not mirrored at local level. Some of Nicaragua's most established NGOs criticise FISE for not respecting existing community organisations and for imposing new organisational structures for their own purposes.

Economic Reform Continues Unchecked

Any contribution the SDA programme has made towards improving policy-making in Mozambique, or that FISE has made towards alleviating some poverty or widening access to some health and education, has to be set within the context of ongoing, and largely unaltered, economic reform policies and practice. The SDA programme did not achieve its objective of incorporating poverty reduction into macro-economic strategy. FISE did not even have this objective.

...they demonstrate the policy-makers' ignorance or neglect of the scale of poverty and its connection with gender inequality...

Both social safety net programmes were conceived as temporary welfare hand-outs. On the one hand, they show some slight recognition on the part of international policy-makers that neo-liberal economic reform programmes have a harsh impact on certain groups. On the other hand, they demonstrate the policy-maker' ignorance or neglect of the scale of poverty and its connection with gender inequality, and their dangerous assumptions that any detrimental social effects will be transitory and that privatised, deregulated and liberalised economies will benefit everyone in the fullness of time.

Poverty in both Mozambique and Nicaragua is intense and widespread. Millions are poor because of the social, economic and political structures which reward the rich and marginalise the poor. The war, and consequent displacement of millions in Mozambique, and tens of thousands in Nicaragua, have exacerbated poverty. Neither the economic reform programmes nor the safety net programmes do anything to enable the poorest women, men and children to live with dignity and enjoy their basic rights.

Richardinha runs a pig slaughtering business in Cape Verde.
(Sue Fleming)

The Informal Economy

For those marginalised from the formal economy — from jobs in the public or private sectors — there are few options but to turn to the informal sector. Faced with high unemployment and a depressed industrial sector, low income households cannot protect their standard of living by increasing the number of wage earners in the formal economy. More and more women and men crowd into the informal economy to become street traders, taxi drivers, collectors of waste paper and bottles for recycling, car windscreen washers, or domestic workers. Traders sell anything they can make or buy. Many sell from door to door or on the side of the street. Others sell in recognised and quite formally organised market places.

The informal sector is growing everywhere. A 1991 survey of households in Maputo, Mozambique, showed that 46 per cent of women are involved in trading of some sort (Fleming, 1993: 7). In Bangladesh the informal sector is becoming more and more crowded. Slum-dwellers in the capital and other large cities work as rickshaw pullers, taxi drivers, cooks, cleaners, food sellers, messengers, waste removers, carriers. They provide essential services but earn barely enough to survive from day to day.

Street trading in Luanda, Angola. (Bob van der Winden)

Nazreen Kanji's (1993) study shows that the informal sector was the most common source of income for women in Zimbabwe. She points out, however, that income from informal sector activities was declining as the sector became more saturated, and as women tended to be involved in the 'most vulnerable, precarious and lowest-paying activities' (1993: 107). As elsewhere, the informal sector in Zimbabwe can include anything from buying and selling food or clothes to doing crotchet or knitting.

The Angolan National Institute of Statistics estimates that women make up 75 per cent of the informal economy and that 80 per cent of all retail transactions are carried out by women. As in other countries, women are found at the bottom of the economy. Interviews with market women in the largest market, Roque Santeiro, in Luanda provide a valuable illustration (Hurlich, 1992; de Andrade, 1995). Most women were supporting seven or eight person households, which on average had at the most two breadwinners. Most women worked six days each week and made a profit of between 40 cents and US$4 per day which was spent on food for their families and working capital to buy goods for selling the next day. Those who borrowed money from a private lender or another family member to start trading paid as much as 20 per cent interest per day. Low profits and inflation made it impossible to accumulate any savings. In the period 1986-90 Roque Santeiro market had about 5,000 traders. By the mid-1990s, it had around 55,000 traders, reflecting the huge numbers displaced from the countryside because of the war and the changes in the formal economy following liberalisation.

The informal sector is a primary site of women's economic activity. But here too, there is a clear hierarchy or economic pyramid. In retail, for example, each level of the pyramid sells smaller and smaller amounts for lower and lower mark-ups. In Angola, the top of the pyramid is in the hands of a small number of importers and wholesalers who are able to obtain foreign exchange at concessionary rates and import licences from government and thus make large profits. The importers and wholesalers import cheaply but sell to small traders at high prices. They enjoy the full benefits of a liberalised and deregulated economy. Women are disproportionately in the lowest levels of the informal economy pyramid.

The informal sector is a primary site of women's economic activity. But here too, there is a clear hierarchy or economic pyramid.

Women cannot compete on an equal footing with men in the informal sector. Women in the Philippines complain that men can start selling earlier in the morning while they are still busy with children and domestic responsibilities. Women in Angola complain of bullying from men over key selling sites. Making some profit in the informal sector is a precarious, marginal, exploitative, time-consuming and isolated endeavour. Earning enough to live on from day to day can take every waking hour. It is particularly difficult to build any kind of organisation to protect group interests. Women, in particular, suffer harassment and violence at the hands of police authorities and self-appointed market bosses.

Activities in the informal economy go well beyond selling and service activities. This is the sector, too, in which all forms of illegal and criminal activities, such as smuggling, drug dealing and prostitution thrive — activities which are closely associated with abuse and violence. The deregulation and liberalisation of economic affairs have allowed these illegal activities to flourish. But they undermine, rather than strengthen economic development. Being outside the mainstream of national economic planning, these transactions largely evade any form of direct taxation and thus deprive the state of much needed revenue.

The informal sector is the response of the poorest women and men to growing poverty; it is their means of staying alive and feeding their children. With all its inequalities, it demonstrates the capacity of the poorest to cope and to adapt to whatever changes are imposed on them.

It shows, too, the incapacity of international policy makers to adjust their policy prescriptions to match reality. The informal economy attracts little attention from governments or aid donors, and women in the informal sector receive very little support in the form of credit, training or protection. Most have to rely on their own knowledge and experience of sales patterns. They have little access to skills, such as accounting, business management, advertising or marketing, which may help them to develop their business. Yet the informal sector is widely acknowledged as the safety net which prevents the poorest from dying or rioting in the streets.

Leaving Home for Work

Poverty, unemployment and low wages at home, coupled with official government encouragement, are pushing more and more Filipino women and men to migrate abroad for work. Over the last five years, migration among women has increased faster than among men. According to official figures, at least 600,000 migrate each year and 60 per cent of these are women. It is estimated that many more migrate through unofficial channels. The ILO estimates that worldwide there are around 100 million economic migrants and refugees including both those who migrate legally and those without legal documentation. Five million of this number are Filipino workers in over 135 countries worldwide. There are an estimated 80,000 Filipino migrant workers in the UK. An analysis of migration from the Philippines and its causes and consequences for migrant workers provides a valuable insight into migration in practice.

Migration has been part of the Philippines government policy since the 1970s. For ex-President Marcos, so-called labour export addressed two major problems facing the economy: unemployment and the balance-of-payments deficit. Labour export in the 1990s, as it did in the 1970s, reduces pressure on the government to create jobs at home and makes a very significant contribution to the Philippines exchequer. Marcos added a third dimension to labour export, namely 'acquisition of skills essential to development of the country's economic base'. It would appear that this dimension was largely window-dressing because Filipino migrant workers are more likely to lose existing skills than acquire new ones. In the early days of labour export no official attention was paid to the welfare of migrants. However, within three years the government was forced to set up mechanisms to provide some social and welfare services, career development services, and other forms of support.

During his presidential election campaign, Fidel V. Ramos promised a manifesto for overseas contract workers. Filipino migrants were promised full citizens' rights to choose to work abroad, to vote and to have their views represented in government. He also pledged that migrants would not suffer double taxation, and promised measures to make it easier for returning workers to 'channel their hard-earned savings into useful endeavours'. There was no commitment to reducing migration; on the contrary, in fact, labour export has become by inference a long-term feature of Philippines economic policy. The economic problems which spurred government to embark on labour export in 1974 still dominate the Philippines today.

Fidel V. Ramos ...promised full citizens' rights to choose to work abroad and pledged that migrants would not suffer double taxation...

The Philippines Overseas Employment Agency (POEA), the government agency handling migration, actively seeks opportunities abroad, recruits contract workers, and offers some orientation, advice, protection and support for those going abroad or returning home. Many Filipinos, however, migrate through other, unofficial, channels.

Demanding, Dirty and Dangerous Work

Apart from a tiny minority of Filipino women and men who migrate from choice to study or work abroad, the overwhelming majority leave home from economic necessity. Most migrants regard work overseas as a temporary measure and intend to return home at some point, even after many years abroad. Most migrants send a high percentage of their income home and try to return on visits as frequently as they can afford and their contracts allow. One survey of migrant women workers carried out by Pertierra (1992) showed that remittances are used to pay for the migrant family's basic needs, to repay debts, finance children's education, and meet housing needs; in addition, a small amount may be saved. Only a few households with a long history of lucrative migration were able to invest in farm inputs or small-scale enterprises. It is estimated that 30 million people are dependent on remittances from migrants (Dico-Young, 1994:19). The remittances benefit the migrant's direct family and ensure its economic survival. There are few long-term benefits to the migrant's wider community in terms of investment in economic development.

Labour-intensive, demanding, dirty and dangerous is how Filipino researchers, Rene E. Ofreneo and Rosalinda Pineda-Ofreneo, characterised the employment of women and men migrant workers in Japan. In recent years, more and more Filipino women and men have migrated to Japan to work as entertainers, construction workers and in other low-paid and labour-intensive jobs in the service and industrial sector — jobs which cannot be relocated overseas. Large numbers of Filipino women and men also migrate to Saudi Arabia (the primary destination country), Kuwait, Europe, the US, and other Asian countries, such as Hong Kong and Singapore.

Of the hundreds of thousands of women who migrate each year, the vast majority become domestic helpers, chambermaids and waitresses. As one writer has put it: 'Hundreds of thousands of Filipinas minister to the personal comfort and convenience of foreign employers the world over while leaving their own children and families to fend for themselves.' Very many women who migrate have professional qualifications as nurses or accountants, for example. Almost half of the 520 overseas contract workers recently surveyed by the Kanlungan Center Foundation had some tertiary education. A Filipino woman can earn more as a domestic worker overseas than as a teacher or other professional at home. By and large, it is the better educated who migrate as they have greater opportunities to raise the fee (10,000-30,000 pesos or $US380-1150 in 1994) necessary to buy a job abroad. In 1990 alone, 28,000 nurses went abroad due to low wages — that is three times the number employed by the Philippines Department of Health. Of these, 4,000 went to the US and 24,000 to the Middle East.

Migrant workers make a significant contribution to the economies of the host countries, whether they are employed as nurses, domestic helpers, construction workers, waitresses or entertainers. This contribution is rarely acknowledged by the host country and in no country are migrant workers given equal workers' rights.

All migrants are vulnerable to exploitative employers and contract violations. The work women migrants do, as domestic helpers and entertainers, has very low social standing and is isolating and personally degrading. Many women experience racial discrimination, physical and mental abuse, and sexual violence. Highest among their complaints are poor accommodation, inadequate food, long hours, loneliness and isolation. The abuse of migrant labourers, particularly domestic workers, by their employers in the UK, in

Saudi Arabia and elsewhere has been well documented and makes shocking reading (see for example, Anderson, 1992; Palma Beltran and Javate de Dios, 1992).

Women migrants who become embroiled in the sex industry as entertainers, bar girls, prostitutes or models for pornography face an array of physical, sexual and psychological abuse. Many are undocumented workers who, without permits and official contracts, are legally non-existent and therefore doubly vulnerable to manipulation and abuse. The Philippine organisations which work with undocumented women migrants use the term 'super-exploitation' to describe the position of these workers who have no legal status and hence no protection. International human rights organisations have described their situation as a form of 'contemporary slavery' (Brennan et al., 1995: 15).

Migrant workers experience a myriad of legal problems. The Kanlungan Center Foundation survey of 520 overseas contract workers showed that 16 per cent experienced problems relating to contract violation, 11 per cent had problems arising from recruitment violations and another 9 per cent faced legal difficulties due to illegal recruitment (TNT, 1993). On arrival overseas to take up their contract, migrant workers all too frequently find the terms and conditions of their employment are not as they were led to believe. Alone in a strange country, many migrants have little option but to accept the situation. In most cases, their work permit and conditions of entry into the country dictate that migrant

Association of Development Agencies, Bangladesh and One World Action Consultation on Structural Adjustment and its effects on women, July 1994, Dhaka, Bangladesh.
(One World Action)

workers complete the number of years stipulated in their contract before they can seek alternative employment.

The conditions migrants face vary from country to country. In some European countries, for example, steps have been taken by migrants themselves to organise and set up Filipino centres, organisations and groups to provide advice and support, as well as social and cultural activities for migrant workers. In May 1991, a group of 10 Filipinas organised themselves to address problems facing migrant workers living in Rome. They founded the Filipino Women's Council (Basa, 1993). A campaigning group in the UK was successful in achieving some legal changes to improve the situation of domestic workers brought into the UK by wealthy individuals as part of their household. These workers had no individual legal status, and were entirely dependent on their employer. Their only recourse from the often slave-like conditions is to run away and thus become illegal immigrants. In other countries, for example, in the Middle East or Asia, migrant workers are not allowed to meet together or to organise. Many countries also strictly forbid women migrants to marry their nationals.

Paying a Heavy Price

The consequences of migration affect the migrant's family, community and country. Maria Teresa Dico-Young (1994) points out the problems of family disintegration and reduced parental authority that can occur due to one parent's long-term absence. Others write of the unquantifiable emotional damage to children which may result. The long-term absence of women from their families means that other family members — aunts, grandmothers, siblings and husbands — take on increased family responsibilities.

The deeper cultural implications of migration are hard to catalogue. Migrant workers undoubtedly take on some of the values of the host country — values which may be at odds with their home culture. There is some evidence, too, that the children of migrants have developed a taste for imported consumer goods (Dico-Young, 1994).

...in a real sense the country's debt burden can be said to fall on the shoulders of the migrant workers. The value of migration to the Philippines economy is unquestioned. Remittances are the largest source of hard currency. Estimates of remittances home from overseas contract workers vary from US$4 billion to US$8 billion annually. IBON, a widely respected research and data bank in Manila, put the figure at US$5.5 billion for 1993. This figure is roughly equivalent to the amount the Philippine government pays each year to service its huge debt of US$34 billion. So, as many Filipinos point out, in a real sense the country's debt burden can be said to fall on the shoulders of the migrant workers. Not content with this large contribution of foreign currency, the Philippine government legislated that overseas contract workers should pay taxes in the Philippines, in addition to paying taxes in the countries where they work and live. Thus, Filipino migrants' income is taxed twice despite promises to the contrary.

The loss to the country's economic development caused by the migration of skilled and professional workers is considerable. The constant and growing brain drain cannot be regarded as positive for the Philippines' long-term development: the vast majority of migrant workers are unlikely to return with their existing skills updated or valuable new skills acquired. The Philippines government objective in promoting overseas contract work, namely, to reduce unemployment at home, has not been met. Unemployment continued to rise in the Philippines in parallel to the rise in migration. As we have seen, it is largely the better educated and more skilled workers who migrate.

The conditions in which most migrant women find themselves are hardly those regarded as synonymous with greater personal advancement or empowerment. Migrants are usually employed in jobs well below their educational qualifications and are predominantly in employment areas which are unprotected, unorganised, and of low economic and social standing (Palma Beltran and Javate de Dios, 1992).

Although women workers from a Southern country who opt for overseas contract work are not motivated by desires of personal liberation, the act of migrating, working abroad, earning an income and contributing significantly to the well-being of her family may increase her personal autonomy and may alter the power relations with her husband. But the personal costs are high. And there is no evidence that returning migrants are keen to organise to challenge the inequality women experience in a more systematic way.

Organisations working with migrants and on migration issues argue for a series of immediate measures to protect the rights of migrant workers now. There have been many successful campaigns in migrant workers' home countries and in the countries where migrants work. Organisations in the Philippines, for example, continue to highlight the situation of migrant women workers, to offer support and advice services and to press for greater protection for migrant workers. Organisations in the UK campaign to protect the rights of migrant workers. All organisations of migrant workers and those involved in migration issues press for longer-term measures to create employment and thus reduce the economic need for women and men to leave their home country. These organisations receive very little official support, especially in Europe.

Migration, and the rights of migrant workers are, above all else, a political matter from which most donor governments turn away.

Conclusion

The situation of street traders in Angola and Filipino migrant workers in Europe are not unique. The informal sector is burgeoning everywhere and the number of economic migrants who go abroad to work is growing in almost all countries in Africa, Asia, Latin America, the Caribbean and, more recently, in East and Central Europe. Everywhere, too, most new jobs are casual, part-time, low-paid, and usually done by women. Homeworking is also on the increase.

The increase in the number of migrant women workers is not an economic abberation. It is yet another manifestation of the international division of labour and the particular place women from Southern countries hold within this. In the same way as easily movable, intensive assembly-line production is exported to Southern countries, Southern workers are 'imported' into Northern countries, often illegally, to fill those jobs which cannot be relocated. The economic irrationality of 'exporting' a country's most highly trained women and men is just one more example of short-term considerations outweighing long-term national development interests.

The sectors of the economy in which the majority of low-income women work are predominately precarious, demanding and ill-rewarded. The jobs open to the poorest women offer few opportunities for personal advancement, and in almost all cases reinforce, rather than challenge, the unequal division of labour between women and men. **The security of assembly-line workers, street traders and migrant workers can only deteriorate as long as deregulation of labour markets and economic affairs rule the day.** The trends towards economic globalisation brought with them a very sophisticated division of labour within which women workers have a particular place ordained by gender, race, class and age. These trends are accelerated by the neo-liberal economic agenda of deregulation and liberalisation, and compound the male-biased hierarchy of economic control and male domination of economic resources.

Side by side with the growth in certain economic sectors comes rising unemployment and so-called jobless growth: increased world income concentrated in fewer hands, accompanied by greater inequalities in wealth distribution. Unemployment is growing everywhere: at the end of 1995, there were around 20 million women and men without waged work in the European Union. The *Human Develop-*

ment Report 1995 (UNDP, 1995) estimates that 1 billion new jobs are needed in developing countries in the next decade. It is not clear from where these jobs will come when the prevailing view is that to increase productivity companies must introduce more labour-saving technology and cut jobs. There are some signs that the belief in 'down-sizing' — cutting jobs — is faltering. Workers must be flexible in order to survive, but flexibility is no guarantee of secure employment.

Changes in employment and income have long-term implications for women's equality and independence. The pressure to cope with the rising cost of living and declining income absorbs more and more of women's time and energy. They are left with little time to take part in community or social organisations outside their home and family or to be active citizens in the building of democracy in their countries. In Chapter Five we move on to look at the political considerations added to the international community's agenda in the 1990s, namely, the emphasis on democratisation and good governance. We examine what these political considerations mean and how they relate to the ongoing economic agenda.

The elections in Angola in 1993 did not bring peace. (Bob van der Winden)

References

Anderson, Bridget. (1992) *Britain's Secret Slaves: an Investigation into the Plight of Overseas Domestic Workers*, London, Anti-Slavery International.

Arcia, Gustavo. (1993) 'The Potential Impact of Structural Adjustment on Nicaragua's Poor and Implications for Safety Net Assistance', Research Triangle Institute (draft).

Basa, Charito. (1993) 'Filipino Women's Council — a Migrant Women's Shelter in Rome' in *Women and Migration*, Women in Action, Nos. 2 & 3, Quezon City, Isis International.

Butler, Judy. (1994) *The Emergency Social Investment Fund (FISE) in Nicaragua: an Evaluation*, London, One World Action.

Brennan, Brid, Vervest, Peitje, and Heijmans, Erik. (1995) 'Asia's Wake up Call to Europe: the Perspectives for the Philippines', Papers for Transnational Institute conference, March 13-14, 1995, Amsterdam.

CWERC (Cordillera Women's Education and Resource Center) and WWP (Women Workers Program). (1994) *Women Workers Situation at the Baguio City Export Processing Zone*, Baguio City, CWERC and WWP.

de Andrade, Henda Ducados Pinto. (1995) *Women, Poverty and the Informal Sector in Luanda's Peri-urban Areas*, Luanda, Development Workshop.

Dico-Young, Maria Teresa. (1994) 'Filipino Women Migrant Workers in the UK: the Impact of Remittances and Changes in Gender Roles on Rural Households in the Philippines', unpublished Special Study prepared for Diploma Course in Rural Extension and Women, University of Reading, UK.

European Community/Philippines 2000 Project, Research papers (draft), Amsterdam, Transnational Institute.

Fleming, Sue. (1993) 'Women on the Side-lines: Policy-making and Poverty in Mozambique', paper prepared for the African Studies Association meeting on Gender and Adjustment in Africa.

Hurlich, Susan. (1992) *Micro Enterprises in Ngola Kiluanje*, Luanda, Development Workshop.

Kanji, Nazreen. (1993) Gender and Structural Adjustment Policies: a Case Study of Harare', unpublished thesis, University of Harare.

Kunzi, Andre. (1994) 'Change and Continuity in Kalinga Status Contests Under the Influence of Outmigration', paper prepared for European Conference on Philippine Studies, School of Oriental and African Studies, University of London, April 13-15 1994.

Laya Women's Collective. (1994) 'Filipinas for export', in *Laya Feminist Quarterly*; Vol. 3, No. 2, Quezon City.

Ofreneo, Rene E. and Pineda-Ofreneo, Rosalinda. (1993) 'The Sex Sector: Prostitution and Development in the Philippines', a revised research report submitted August 1993.

Ofreneo, Rene E. and Pineda-Ofreneo, Rosalinda. (1991) 'Filipino Workers in Japan: Caught in an Unequal Global Division of Labour', paper presented at the symposium on Japanese Economy and Migrant Workers from Abroad, October 12, 1991, at Kanagawa University, Yokohama, Japan.

One World Action/CISAS. (1994) 'El Impacto de las Reformas Económicas en las Mujeres Nicaragüenses,' report of consultation held on August 23, 1994 in Managua.

Palma Beltran, Ruby and Javate de Dios, Aurora (eds). (1992) *Filipino Women Overseas Contract Workers ... At What Cost?*, Quezon City, Women in Development Foundation Inc. and Goodwill Trading Co. Limited.

Pertierra, R. (ed.). (1992) *Remittances and Returnees: the Culture and Economy of Migration in Ilocos*, Quezon City, New Day Publishers.

Renzi, María Rosa et al. (1994) *Impacto de los Proyectos FISE en las Condiciones de Vida de los Nicaragüenses*, FIDEG, Managua.

Schubert, B. (1993) 'Social Assistance to Destitute Urban Households as Part of the Social Safety Net in Mozambique', cited in Bridget M. Walker and Gabriel L. Dava. (1994), *The Social Dimensions of Adjustment (SDA) Initiative in Mozambique: an Evaluation*, London, One World Action.

SDA Steering Committee. (1993) *The Social Dimensions of Adjustment Program: a General Assessment*, Washington, World Bank.

TNT (Trends, News & Tidbits). (1994) 'Feminization of Migration', in *TNT*, newsletter of Kanlungan Center Foundation, Inc., Issue No. 6, Quezon City, January–March.

TNT (Trends, News & Tidbits). (1993) 'Philippines 2000 and the OCWs', in *TNT*, newsletter of Kanlungan Center Foundation, Inc., Issue No. 5, Quezon City, December.

United Nations. (1991) *The World's Women: Trends and Statistics 1970–1990,* New York, United Nations.

UNDP (United Nations Development Programme). (1995) *Human Development Report 1995,* Oxford and New York, Oxford University Press.

United Nations. (1991) *The World's Women: Trends and Statistics 1970–1990,* New York, United Nations.

Walker, Bridget M. and Dava, Gabriel L. (1994) *The Social Dimensions of Adjustment (SDA) Initiative in Mozambique: an Evaluation,* London, One World Action.

5. Good Governance: Completing the Picture?

As the Cold War ended in the very late 1980s, new political considerations were added to the international development agenda. Good governance, democratisation and respect for human rights have figured prominently in international policy statements ever since. The concentration on economic liberalism which had dominated North-South relations since the early 1980s was extended to include political liberalisation. After a short overview of the various policies, this chapter will discuss how the political and economic agendas fit together and then look behind the policy statements and see what is happening in practice. It concludes by making the case for a broader and deeper view of good governance and democracy.

If we ask why good governance arrived on the international agenda, several possible answers present themselves. The end of the Cold War enabled Northern donor governments to redefine their relationship with Southern countries. In short, Northern governments and institutions were no longer compelled by expediency to support, or respect the autonomy of, authoritarian and oppressive regimes in the South. The USSR's centrally planned economy and authoritarian regime were discredited utterly. The free market model of economic life and democratic rule were victorious.

There were other considerations too: the economic reform process had failed to deliver stable or sustainable economic development in any Southern country. One explanation in the minds of the international financial institutions and donor governments was that Southern governments were inefficient and unaccountable, and therefore their economies were badly managed. There was no shortage of evidence of growing military expenditure alongside cuts in basic services, inefficient state-owned enterprises and corruption. In short, structural adjustment programmes were not working because they had not been implemented properly. Sound administration and liberal political regimes would complete the picture.

There is yet another dimension to the new interest in political liberalisation. The North's greater objective of integrating the economies of the South into the global economy is advanced significantly by the promotion and installation of compatible political systems in the South. It is believed that regimes based on some form of multiparty electoral democracy are unlikely to instigate revolutionary economic or social programmes and upset the neo-liberal project.

While we should not overlook the North's greater objectives, it would be inaccurate to dismiss the whole good governance agenda as merely part of a grand conspiracy. Good governance is a valid and desirable objective in itself. It is also important as a means towards achieving more equitable economic and social justice. It is also, as the UK's Overseas Development Administration (ODA) points out, 'a necessary condition for effective use of aid' (albeit, a condition neglected until the 1990s).

Good governance is a valid and desirable objective in itself.

Anti-violence against women poster, Bangladesh.

Good Governance

In October 1993, the ODA issued a Technical Note, entitled *Taking Account of Good Government* (ODA, 1993). This was the ODA's first attempt at fleshing out the practical implications of earlier UK government statements on the subject. The Note sets out the agenda of good governance as including the following overlapping elements:

- the legitimacy of government, which depends on the existence of participatory processes and the consent of the those who are governed;
- the accountability of both the political and official elements of government for their actions depending on the availability of information, freedom of the media, transparency of decision-making and the existence of mechanisms to call individuals and institutions to account;
- the competence of government to formulate appropriate policies, make timely decisions, implement them effectively and deliver services;
- respect for human rights and the rule of law guaranteeing individual and group rights and security, to provide a framework for economic and social activity and to allow and encourage all individuals to participate.

Good governance as so outlined is an impressive agenda founded on respect for certain principles, such as human rights (political and civil at least — it is less clear on social, economic and cultural rights), and on certain concepts such as multiparty democracy. The ODA, alongside other donors, sees multiparty democracy as offering 'the best way of ensuring legitimacy'. It acknowledges that in certain circumstances a multiparty system may not be practical or sustainable and in such cases ' other means of consulting and being responsive to the needs of the people as a whole' are necessary to meet the criteria of legitimacy. A healthy civil society, that is, 'a range of institutions outside government which represent other interests and provide a counterweight to the power of government', is regarded as a critical element in legitimacy. A healthy civil society includes trade unions, business associations, women's organisations, community groups, professional bodies, and the media.

The ODA was not alone in developing ideas on good governance. In 1993, the World Bank published *Getting Results: the World Bank's Agenda for Improving Development Effectiveness*; this was the Bank's response to the criticisms made in the 1992 Wapenhans' (Wapenhans 1992) report which drew attention to problems in the Bank's performance and effectiveness in poverty reduction, its stated primary aim. While regarding the strictly political issues of elections and government legitimacy as outside its brief, the Bank had a great interest in sound administration, competent government and what it called 'ownership'. The commitment of borrowing governments to development operations, and the degree of 'ownership' assumed by them, were regarded as critical to the success or failure of any particular initiative. Strengthening 'ownership' called for a genuine partnership, a 'more systematic analysis of how different constituencies will be affected', greater involvement of 'effective, local NGOs', and 'efforts to encourage broad, meaningful participation and leadership by both government and private agencies ... throughout the project cycle' (World Bank, 1993: 12).

For its part the Bank set itself the challenge '... to change the ways it interacts with borrowers, from a pattern dominated by prescription, imposition, condition-setting and decision-making to one characterised by explanation, demonstration, facilitation, and advice' (World Bank, 1993: 12). This was proof in retrospect, if proof were needed, that indebted developing countries had little choice but to install harsh economic reform programmes.

The European Union, too, made clear its position. The Maastricht Treat (European Union, 1992) sets out the objectives of its development cooperation. Community policy, in the sphere of development cooperation, 'shall foster the sustainable economic and social development of the developing countries, and particularly the most disadvantaged among them'; shall foster 'the smooth and gradual integration of the developing counties into the world economy'; shall foster 'the campaign against poverty in the developing countries'; and shall 'contribute to the general objectives of developing and consolidating democracy and the rule of law, and to that of respecting human rights and fundamental freedoms.'

Other European governments have also endorsed the political agenda. In 1991, the Dutch government set out the objectives of development cooperation in the 1990s. It gave priority to freedom, democracy and human rights as preconditions for socio-economic development which benefits the entire population. In 1995, the Swedish Government announced its development policy for world solidarity, security and democracy. Swedish development cooperation would be used, the policy stated, to support the transition to peace and democracy and to prevent the outbreak of conflicts. It would aim to strengthen democratic structures and protect human rights.

Engendering Good Governance

Gender differences determine to a very large extent the real experience of women and men, and their interests, and thus their ability to have their interests represented.

The initial good governance agenda, like most others adopted by the international community in relation to Southern countries, paid little attention to gender inequality. The elements of good governance — legitimacy, accountability, transparency, and respect for human rights — were assumed to be gender-neutral concepts. As Duckworth (1995) wrote, '... donors have assumed that the programmes they are supporting to enhance the accountability of political leaders will ensure that the interests of both men and women are better represented'. Some progress has been made since to clarify the gender dimensions of the good governance agenda. However, encouraging Southern governments to become more accountable, more competent and more transparent does not necessarily ensure they are better at respecting and promoting women's rights unless that is an explicit objective of both donor and Southern governments.

...encouraging Southern governments to become more accountable... does not necessarily ensure they are better at respecting and promoting women's rights.

The effects of 'bad governance' is increased poverty amongst women. Poverty, as Ashworth (1994) asserted, is manifested in every aspect of life: lack of right to property, land and other assets which provide protection and security and the means to earn a livelihood. It is seen too in women's universal lower earnings and the imbalances of women's power relative to men in every sphere. Institutional discrimination and constitutional inequality, together with multiplying forms of random and systematic violence by men against women in public and private, are further evidence of 'bad governance'. Ashworth questions the legitimacy of governments which '... are composed of a minority (males) without representation of, or accountability to, the majority (females)' (Ashworth, 1994: 63). For the most part women's consent is assumed. This is not to argue that women in government automatically represent women's gender interests but to emphasise that concepts such as legitimacy, competence and accountability need to be analysed from a gender perspective.

An Uneasy Partnership

Economic and political liberalisation are uneasy partners. One of the basic tenets of structural adjustment programmes is limiting the role of the state in economic and social affairs. In practice, in many Southern countries, the state's role in managing the economy has been sharply reduced through deregulation and privatisation; the belief is that less state equals good state. The cutting back of public spending in such areas as the civil service and public services, such as health and education, has diminished the capacity of most Southern states to deliver basic services. Thus, in the context of harsh economic reform, it is difficult, if not impossible, for governments to be good to their citizens.

The ways in which the economic reform programmes were introduced, at the behest of the international financial institutions and donor governments, and only rarely with electoral mandate or public consultation, undermine government legitimacy. As poverty increases, so does social instability, and usually crime too. The consequent increase in policing and use of repressive measures to maintain law and order lead inevitably to human rights abuses. In response to rising protests and food riots, many governments have turned to increased repression, thus further damaging their legitimacy and accountability.

A critical point when discussing good governance is that, as we have seen, neo-liberal economic policy and practice are premised on inequality between women and men. It is assumed that women will continue to carry family and domestic responsibilities, that women will pick up any shortfalls coming from reduced public services, that women will accept (because they have little alternative) lower wages, and that women, because of their family responsibilities and lack of resources, cannot easily take up arms to overthrow unrepresentative and unresponsive governments. As Duckworth (1995: 5) writes: '... as long as a gender division of labour exists in society, it is women (particularly the poorest) who lose out most when "government accountability" stops short of protecting citizens' social and economic rights.'

Economic reform has hampered political accountability in other ways too. A central element of the good governance agenda is a healthy civil society composed of trade unions, women's organisations and other associations. Here again the donors' economic and political agendas appear to be at odds with each other. The deregulation of the economy involves the removal of all constraints on the operation of the market. Collective bargaining agreements, health and safety standards, even trade union organisation itself, are perceived as constraints on the market. Governments in many countries, North and South alike, are taking, or have taken, steps to limit trade union activity. The combination of redundancies, or the threat of redundancies, and rising unemployment and deregulation serve to undermine the strength and role of trade unions, often amongst the largest and most coherent civil society organisations.

What of Genuine Democracy?

The capacity of women and men to perform as political actors is severely limited by poverty and the daily struggle to survive. With growing divides between poor and rich within Northern and Southern countries, and between women and men, it is clear that millions of people are effectively disenfranchised. In Dhaka, the capital of Bangladesh, millions of semi-permanent urban slum dwellers do not have voting rights. In the UK, thousands of homeless women and men are not on the electoral register. To the millions of women, men and children living in poverty, who have little opportunity to exercise their human rights, a good government is surely one which protects the most marginalised, which manages the country's resources in such as way as to ensure all citizens have access to the means of livelihood and basic services, and 'can achieve equality in their daily lives' (Duckworth, 1995: 4).

This is so, even in the established liberal democracies. For many, political participation begins and ends with casting a vote at election time. What do free and fair elections and universal suffrage mean in the context of extreme poverty where a promised vote may mean the difference between improved short-term survival or not? This is not to devalue the importance of exercising one's electoral democratic rights; it is, however, to indicate the need for a wider definition of democracy and governance. Critics of liberal democracy stress that having the right to express one's interests and register one's vote does not guarantee an equal influence on political decisions.

With rising poverty and unemployment, especially among women, and little capacity on the part of the state to intervene or to deliver basic services, it is hard to imagine how good governance, not to mention social cohesion and law and order, will be advanced.

Exporting Democracy

The international community's commitment to political liberalisation is quite limited in practice. It appears content with the occurrence of occasional multiparty elections which it gladly supports and remains unconcerned with a genuinely democratic culture in the family, in the workplace, or at local and national level. Goodison (1994: 51) contends that there is a tendency within the European Union to see democracy as an event rather than a process. Relatively few resources are allocated to measures which would enable democracy to survive, flourish and permeate all levels of society. While building and strengthening democratic and accountable structures throughout societies is on the donor's agenda, this stated interest is not matched with substantial resources. The international community seems happy to export and, to a large extent, impose top-down democracy, as the case of Mozambique below demonstrates. Countries in Africa come under much greater international pressure with regard to democracy and good governance than countries in Asia or in the Middle East; it would seem that the greater the trading opportunities, the less pressure for political reform. The poverty of most African countries, and their

...a good government is surely one which protects the most marginalised, which manages the country's resources in such as way as to ensure all citizens have access to the means of livelihood and basic services...

Relatively few resources are allocated to measures which would enable democracy to survive, flourish and permeate all levels of society.

restricted possibilities for rapid progress towards good governance, are not taken into account. The World Bank does not appear to apply its notion of 'ownership' to political development.

While the majority of donors may be convinced in principle about the importance of good governance, this is not reflected accurately in their practice or expenditure patterns. Funds for long-term development are under pressure: global aid flows are falling, emergency relief and programme (balance of payments) aid are given prominence; and much aid is diverted to the countries of the former Soviet Union.

Over and above all of this, most donors have non-aid objectives for their aid budgets: these are mainly commercial, but also strategic, objectives which frequently overrule all other considerations. These are observable when we examine the extent to which the UK or other donors do use aid as a lever to promote civil and political rights or, more accurately, to prevent the blatant abuse of those rights. Here again, there seems to be a direct correlation between donors' own commercial interests and the degree to which they are willing to raise civil and political rights issues. For example, the UK's commercial interests in India will take precedence over any consideration of rights. Sudan, on the other hand, can expect harsh criticism of its record. Social, economic and cultural rights do not figure much in the international donor community's dialogue with Southern governments; nor does their abuse arouse much response in the form of persuasion, pressure or sanctions.

The case of the European Union and the Lomé IV Mid-Term Review throws up some other interesting dilemmas. In *Horizon 2000* the European Union drew particular attention 'to the universality and indivisibility of human rights and the obligation of all States to respect them'. It stressed 'the important role of development assistance in promoting both economic, social, cultural rights as well as civil and political liberties by means of representative democratic government based on respect for human rights' (European Union, 1992). However, in the Lomé IV Mid-Term Review process the European Union worked to redefine the relationship with the African, Caribbean and Pacific (ACP) group of countries in a way that would undermine their capabilities to be accountable and responsive to their citizens. The Lomé agreements are based on the idea of cooperation: the ACP countries would provide the administrative and policy framework for development cooperation activities, and the EU would provide financial and technical cooperation. In the Mid-Term Review, the EU took steps to centralise all decision-making about development cooperation in Europe. The European Union's commitment to good governance and human rights is a qualified one.

Is liberal political reform compatible with neo-liberal economic reform and are these mutually supportive? Does the international donor community's concern with democracy stop at formal multiparty democracy, that is, elections? The most important question of all, perhaps, is whether the concern to advance democratisation is helped or hindered by other policy priorities. The experiences of Mozambique and Zimbabwe provide some answers.

Meeting to discuss democracy and voting in Eritrea. (Jenny Matthews)

Zimbabwe: Whose Economic Reform Programme?

In 1991, Zimbabwe began an IMF/World Bank-style economic structural adjustment programme (ESAP). Zimbabwe was in fact already following very conservative financial policies on currency valuation and balance of payments. It was not in arrears with its debt repayments, it had not asked for debt rescheduling and it had an average growth rate of 4 per cent. There is disagreement among commentators as to why Zimbabwe joined the neo-liberal economic club. Some argue that the government came under intense international financial pressure: Stoneman (1993), for example, asserts that the World Bank and the IMF desperately needed an African structural adjustment 'success story'. Others see the government's implementation of ESAP as stemming from internal decisions.

In any case, there was no consultation or public debate about ESAP and no transparency or accountability about the decision. What is more, ESAP has the effect of making the Zimbabwean government less capable of delivering basic services to the Zimbabwean people. ESAP also led the government to take steps which may in the long term undermine its legitimacy and democratic nature. The changes which ESAP brought in labour relations illustrate this point.

The true democracy is employment, mural in Managua, Nicaragua.
(Jenny Matthews)

Throughout the 1980s, relations between the organised labour movement and the Zimbabwe state had been relatively cooperative; the labour movement had endorsed the government's social programme and had secured safeguards for employment security. Relations deteriorated with the introduction of ESAP. From the perspective of the

Zimbabwe Congress of Trade Unions (ZCTU), the government introduced radically new social and economical policies without any national debate or consultation with important social partners such as the union movement. The government did invite ZCTU to participate in a committee to discuss the implementation of the Social Development Fund, set up as a safety net for those affected by ESAP, and another to discuss labour law changes. But ZCTU's views on ESAP as a whole were neither solicited nor welcomed.

ZCTU has been vocal in its opposition to ESAP since its introduction. It organised protest marches about changes to the Labour Relations Act and about rising living costs. A day of action organised by ZCTU during 1993 was prevented by a government show of strength (Woodroffe, 1993). The Congress used the media whenever possible to criticise ESAP as unjust and unworkable. The trade unions also took action to challenge job losses: numerous disputes arose as unions argued for workers' redundancy rights. In some cases, Works Councils were able to avoid retrenchment by negotiating a shorter working week and revised benefits. There were cases in which unions embarked on legal battles to oppose the cut-backs.

The trade union movement was weakened directly in a number of ways. A central objective of ESAP was to create flexibility for employers and thus rescind the legal provisions which guaranteed employment security. The deregulation of labour conditions side by side with rising unemployment, or unemployment threats, had an immediate effect on relations between workers and their employers. The loss of members due to rising unemployment weakened individual trade unions and the union movement in general. In the context of insecurity about the future, many workers and their unions felt unable to press their case for pay rises to match rising prices or to resist changes to their workloads; this insecurity, and the fact that for each vacancy there would be many applicants, allowed many employers to adopt a 'take it or leave it' attitude towards their workforce. The Labour Relations Act was amended to increase ministerial power to set maximum wages, to remove the 'one industry, one union' policy, to restrict industrial action, and to give more priority to the Works Councils. Speaking about the findings of a survey of clothing and textile workers carried out in 1993, the Acting Secretary General of the Zimbabwe Congress of Trade Unions summed up the situation as follows:

> 'Employers victimised workers, threatened them with retrenchment if they made reasonable demands, engaged contract workers because they were weak, cut benefits, made incentive targets that were impossible to meet and

weakened the unions by not recognising them at the shop-floor.' (ZCTU, 1993: 16)

Trade unions are not the only civil society grouping in Zimbabwe to find their views on ESAP unwelcome. In 1991, student demonstrations for increased grants to cover the cost of living were met with riot police. A new human rights organisation, ZIM Rights, and the media were accused by the Minister of National Security of 'sowing the seeds of despondency and conflict' in 1992 (Kanji, 1993: 177). Members of Parliament who questioned government policy were warned by the President and the Speaker of 'taking democracy too far' in 1992. Discussions on curbing press freedom were held at cabinet level during 1992. Allegations of harassment and intimidation of editors and journalists were numerous (Kanji, 1993: 177-8).

Sithembiso Nyoni, an NGO activist, says that ESAP disempowers both government and people. She lists a number of elements of ESAP which are inherently undemocratic:

> It deprives citizens of their rights to participate in economic matters of their countries... It removes economic power not only from the people but also from their elected governments to faceless private actors, thus disempowering both government and the people... ESAP violates human rights particularly in poor communities. Employment, education, health services and participation are some of the basic human rights. The poor, particularly women and youth, are denied these rights (1993: 11-14).

ESAP in Zimbabwe has unwittingly opened up more political space for interest groups to organise. The imposition of ESAP without consultation and the repressive nature of government response to criticism have demolished any traces of 'a social contract' while the rising costs of living and unemployment have provided the impetus and the opportunity for some social movements to grow in strength. These developments in civil society have to be seen in the wider context of growing poverty, a reduction in the state's power to shape economic and social policy, a weakening of the trade union movement, and a strong sense of political, social and economic instability.

Mozambique: the New Colonialism
(Research and documentation by Beverley Duckworth)

The situation of Mozambique highlights yet more policy inconsistencies. The elections which took place in Mozambique in October 1994 were at the behest, and on the cheque book, of the international donors. The UN sent a force of

7,000, including military and police, to Mozambique in the run-up to the elections at a cost of about US$1 million per day. The UN special representative, Aldo Ajello, was the most powerful man in the country in the months preceding the elections (Brittain, 1994).

After years of protracted negotiations, and with majority rule in South Africa in view, a peace agreement was signed between the Mozambican government and Renamo, the rebels backed by the then South African regime. The international community, particularly the US and South Africa, played a key role in advising Renamo in the negotiating process and in ensuring that multiparty elections were part of the peace settlement. The new constitution introduced in 1990 formally opened the way for a multiparty system with provisions for universal suffrage and a secret ballot. The constitution separates the executive, legislative and judicial branches of government and enshrines freedom of the press and the right to strike. Renamo received US$20 million from the UN to transform itself into a political party. This generosity was explained by the UN's belief that this was the only way to guarantee an end to the fighting and the involvement of Renamo in the electoral process. Other donors funded Frelimo and a range of emerging small political parties.

Throughout the transition period and especially in the immediate run-up to the election, the international community made it very clear that the desired outcome was a government of national unity. With its support, Renamo obtained an effective veto in the election process and, against government wishes, an electoral law which kept all the smaller parties out of parliament.

Engendering Elections

Victoria Brittain (1994) quoted one UN figure as saying...'the one thing this isn't is democracy and individual votes — in the rural areas people will vote as their community leaders tell them'. The Mozambique presidential and legislative elections threw up some interesting gender-related issues. Considerable efforts were made by the registration teams to ensure that women registered to vote. Civil education through the use of posters, role play, radio and other media played an important role, assisted greatly by the various women's organisations whose strong community-based structures gave them access to women (Jacobson, 1994). It is not possible to know what percentage of women registered as no systematic gender-disaggregated breakdown was done (Jacobson, 1994). Turn-out at the elections would seem to indicate that a high percentage of women registered. While the total percentage of women candidates in the 13 parties was around 14 per cent, it was much higher for

Frelimo, at 37 per cent; 9 per cent of Renamo's candidates were women. Following the election, women constituted 24.4 per cent of the legislature.

In the election campaigns both large parties, Frelimo and Renamo, claimed to be the party of democracy which would bring peace and development. Both kept well within the confines of orthodox economic reform but did promise investment in health and education. The issue of most critical relevance to the vast majority of women — that of land rights — was avoided. Land was regarded as too contentious and peace-threatening to handle (Jacobson, 1994). Both Frelimo and Renamo also promoted themselves as the party of traditional values and emphasised women's family responsibilities.

More, or Less, Democracy?

The new freedoms guaranteed in the constitution (free market capitalism and political pluralism) may allow Mozambicans to play a more active part in running their country, but sceptics have warned that replacing the remains of the participatory form of representation of social movements by a more formal individual representation could act to alienate the majority of Mozambicans from the democratic process. The tradition of popular participation and consultation, however limited and imperfect in the early days of independence, has been abandoned. Politics could become the exclusive domain of professional politicians representing privileged social groups (Bowen, 1992). In fact, some analysts argue that the condition of the state, economy and security in Mozambique could mean that more political parties at this time will have some negative effects, such as the diversion of resources that could have been used for rehabilitation and development, significant benefits being captured by elites, and increased internal division.

The state in Mozambique, still fragile due to the colonial inheritance, was decimated by the war of destabilisation, the economic reform process, and by the pressures of mounting poverty. One of the conditions of democracy is an efficient state, one which is accountable and competent. The state in Mozambique, still fragile due to the colonial inheritance, was decimated by the war of destabilisation, the economic reform process, and by the pressures of mounting poverty. This fragility was worsened by the donors' heavy involvement in the day-to-day running of the country, combined with their intimate participation in the election process which further undermined the state's power and capacity to govern. While it would be wrong to underestimate the shortcomings of the state before the donors arrived, it must be remembered that a stated objective of most donors is to strengthen institutional capacity, transfer skills and offer training. Once again it seems the international community acted on instincts which overrode policy commitments:

Legislative and presidential elections in Zambezia province, Mozambique, 1994. (Anders Gunnartz/ Panos Pictures)

antipathy to the Frelimo one-party state system, and unquestioning adherence to untrammelled neo-liberal economics.

The state has lost most of its autonomy in decision-making and with it much of its legitimacy in the eyes of the population. It no longer has an active role in guiding and managing the economy and it has been rendered incapable of delivering even basic services. Health care, for example, is almost completely in the hands of the donor community since the government has no resources to run a health service. In 1994, the donors were financing 50 per cent of the health sector's recurrent expenditure and 80 per cent of drug imports (Hermele, 1990). It is still an inadequate service.

If the international donor community were supporting effectively reconstruction and long-term development one might excuse its hands-on approach. The donors all have their own priorities and procedures for channelling aid and, contrary to government wishes, emergency assistance has been growing significantly in proportion to development assistance (Hermele, 1990). This has occurred despite the fact that short-term relief has become an increasingly inappropriate and clearly ineffective strategy for resolving the long-term nature of Mozambique's 'emergency'. The continued use of food aid is a case in point. The US, for example, continued to bring yellow maize from the US into Mozambique as food aid rather than use its resources to transport and distribute local stocks of maize.

The sheer number of donors alone made it impossible for the state to coordinate their aid programmes into any coherent strategy. But despite the fact that the donors have found Mozambique's systems for coordinating emergency or development assistance inadequate and frustrating, there has been little willingness on their part to support and strengthen the government capacities (Hermele, 1990). Indeed, some donors have taken it upon themselves to bypass state structures altogether. The establishment of donor structures which operate in parallel with the official system effectively weakens the government, further adds to difficulties in planning and makes future dependence on the donors who set up those structures inescapable (Brochmann and Ofstad, 1990).

Thousands of women demonstrated in Dhaka, Bangladesh in April 1994 to protest against Islamic clerics' attempts to ban pro-women NGOs.
(Pavel Rahman/AP)

The end result is that Mozambique is locked into a new dependency. The state is no longer in control of the country's destiny, the Mozambican people do not know in any real sense who is running the country and have no means of making the donors accountable to them. Mozambique is more dependent than it was before 1975, but its donors are more free than the ex-colonial power. As Plank (1993) points out, the relationships that this new colonialism implies are not offset by the traditional responsibilities of a colonial power. In one sense, however, the donors are not free: while they retain their formal power to reduce or cut off assistance, the depth of the country's misery and the government's prompt compliance with their policy conditionalities make it difficult for them to withdraw (Plank, 1993: 421).

The imposition of Western-style multiparty elections on countries, like Mozambique, called for a nation-wide crash course in electoral democracy. The concepts of universal suffrage, secret ballots and free individual voting choice were unfamiliar concepts in the political consciousness of most Mozambicans, particularly in the more remote rural areas. That so many participated in the election process is an indication of Mozambicans' desire for peace and the greater economic security this promised. The long-term benefits of this participation are unclear. It remains to be seen how well women can express their demands and how well these are responded to with government action. Democracy in Mozambique, particularly for women, requires an ongoing commitment to direct external and internal resources towards strengthening women's organisations, towards education and training, including legal and other kinds of literacy, and programmes which support and protect women's economic, social and political rights, and towards strengthening institutions at a local level, which would be accessible to all citizens, especially women. Mozambican women farmers need access to, and control over, land. They need easy access to credit, information and technology. Without these basic essentials they are unlikely to be in a position to demand accountability from government structures. Women in the urban areas require similar forms of support. The presence of this active support, or not, is the true test of democracy and good governance.

Conclusions

Many Southern (and Northern) countries are not well managed. The colonial legacy left many developing countries and their people with minimal administrative structures and experience. Many countries find it difficult to keep trained and qualified women and men at home to run the country when bright lights and better opportunities signal from abroad. For many countries, particularly in Africa, the period from independence to the debt crisis and the consequent stringent economic reforms was less than two decades. This is not to excuse the occurrence of corruption. Many governments have found themselves forced from their chosen path to development by externally-backed wars, as in the case of Nicaragua, Mozambique and Angola, or by external financial pressure. Governments, and the legitimacy they possessed whether through popular revolution or election, have found themselves undermined by external donor interference and conflicting donor demands.

As the examples in this chapter have demonstrated there is a considerable incoherence in the international community's agenda between economic and political concerns. A good government should ensure its country's citizens can live in security, can earn a living, have somewhere to live and have access to health care, education and other essentials. A good government in the eyes of the international financial institutions could be characterised as one which allows the country's economy to operate freely according to market forces, cuts back public spending in health care, education and housing, repays its external debts, keeps workers pliant to attract foreign investment, and keeps political opposition and media criticism at bay through repression or bullying. A good government in neo-liberal economic terms is unlikely to create long-term stability or security. Writing about Bangladesh, Atiur Rahman (1994), reiterates this point:

> Given such a wide variety of social costs, SAP remains vulnerable to the challenges from those who have been marginalised. It is true that right today they lack political strength. But who can guarantee that, they will never get together to challenge SAP more politically? The current passivity should not be construed as strength of policy reforms.

Bangladesh has continued to invest in the police and to increase spending on various instruments of internal repression to ensure some order as the economic reforms undermine democracy.

The economic reforms have had the effect of devaluing politicians and political processes as more and more important decisions are taken outside Southern countries. Liberalisation and deregulation have increased the power of transnational companies and international finance. As we have seen, it is they who decide where to invest, what to produce and the terms of trade. Elected politicians have less and less authority or capacity to decide on national priorities. Ironically, this has facilitated the entrenchment of power in the hands of rich elites; it has reinforced cronyism in some countries and the trade in political and economic patronage. The result is increasing alienation of women and men from political processes.

Liberalisation and deregulation have increased the power of transnational companies and international finance.

Governments and their administrations require considerable investment and support to become responsible, competent, transparent and legitimate. Were sufficient resources allocated to it, genuine aid could assist this process. But with aid budgets declining throughout the North, and the growing reverse flows from South to North in the form of debt repayments and interest, it is difficult not to be sceptical about the Northern donors' commitment to fostering good governance and democracy. The unhindered and flourishing trade in arms and repression technology, so vital to the economies of the North, alongside pro-democracy policy statements, adds to one's scepticism.

There is another element of hypocrisy, too, and a narrowness and ethnocentrism, in the good governance agenda. The way in which the agenda is implemented exposes its promoters to the charge of being highly selective in responding to abuses of civil and political rights; the part played by trade interests is obvious. On the other hand, they neglect social, economic and cultural rights. Yet the indivisibility of rights — civil and political, social, economic and cultural — is now widely acknowledged and their equal importance is accepted in international law. In 1986, the UN General Assembly adopted the Declaration on the Right to Development which recognises that every human person and all peoples are entitled to participate in, contribute to, and enjoy economic, social, cultural, and political development (Hausermann, 1994).

The universality of rights is also stronger in commitment than in action. The rights of women in all countries, of the poorest groups, of indigenous peoples and of ethnic minorities are abused on a daily basis as a result of government policy and development practice. In this respect, donors, international financial institutions and Southern governments are equally culpable. It is not possible for women to achieve equality in the midst of growing poverty, unemployment and decimated essential services. The Declaration and Platform for Action agreed in Beijing in September 1995 at the UN Fourth World Conference on Women reiterated that it was the duty of all governments to ensure women could enjoy and exercise their full human rights.

In Mozambique, for example, although the constitution enshrines the equality of women and men, equal rights legislation lags seriously behind. The laws on work, for example, appear to protect women, but the majority of women workers are peasants who cannot benefit from these laws (CEA/FEMNET, 1992). Equal rights legislation, though important in itself and a powerful indication of government intent, means little in practice in times of widespread poverty. For women to enjoy their rights it is required that governments, and donors, give priority to creating the conditions in which they can effectively exercise them.

Ashworth (1994) elaborated some recommended commitments and changes: policy commitment at all levels, equality legislation, and confronting biases in language and information. The gender dimensions in public life must be addressed, including a total review of the operations of the judiciary and the police, and measures to facilitate women's participation in decision-making processes and institutions. Active policies to prevent different forms of male violence against women in public and private are critical. These are useful scales by which we can measure the activities of Northern and Southern governments.

It is not possible for indigenous peoples to enjoy their rights when, as in the Philippines, their ancestral lands are taken over and devastated by large-scale mining, as we have seen in Chapter Three. One of the greatest challenges facing a government is how it protects the rights of minority and other marginalised groups; it is also one of the indicators of good governance. As Joji Cariño (1994: 35-36) writes:

> Focusing on indigenous peoples allows a view of governance from the lens of the most disenfranchised in society, giving rise to serious challenges to the very concepts of governance, of development, of security, and of the measures necessary to resolve existing conflicts between governments and marginalised groups.

Governance involves the relationship of government and governed — all those governed; not only the elite, or those who supported the winning party and/or leader. The links between political democracy and economic democracy are critical here. All groups and individuals must be guaranteed a minimum level of economic security in order that they can be active participants in political and economic decision-making.

Electoral democracy, without genuine democracy in social, economic and political affairs and a commitment to gender equality and social justice, may result in sham democracy. Mengisteab and Logan (1995: 92) argue that unless the notion of democracy in Africa is expanded, 'its potential for improving human conditions, fostering socio-economic development and resolving the multitude of chronic conflicts that have plagued the continent will be severely undermined'.

There are also specific concerns associated with the issues around the protection of each individual worker's rights. Diane Elson (1991) compares human resources to natural resources. In both cases, the long-term developmental implications should be uppermost. It is wholly irrational, in Elson's view, to deplete human resources on the pretext that poor countries cannot afford the luxury of good labour standards. In order to democratise production, legislation on workers' rights and workers' organisations to defend those rights and respect for the agreed ILO conventions are essential safeguards; these are particularly critical with regard to women workers and their rights. The EU itself has a Social Chapter within the Maastrict Treaty on workers' rights.

The European Union's June 1995 policy statement on structural adjustment demonstrates a recognition that economic affairs cannot be separated from political and social. It states that the EU policy on economic reform must be coherent with its obligations with regard to 'developing and consolidating democracy and the rule of law, and to that of respecting human rights and fundamental freedoms' as set out in Article 130u of the Maastricht Treaty.

The good governance agenda raises very large questions about the nature and form of democracy and its relationship to development. Many writers have been critical of the international community's new-found interest in democracy and their apparent demarcation of the debate in terms of mutiparty electoral democracy. They are critical, too, of the donors' own lack of transparency about the shortcomings of electoral democracy in their own countries and the donors' own lack of accountability to their citizens. Funding multiparty elections, as the donors did in Mozambique, is important, but one election does not guarantee another or create active democracy.

Looking back on around five years of policy development and practice in implementing the good governance agenda, some donor governments are recognising the complexity of the change required: good governance is not merely a technical matter; it requires significant attitudinal changes on all sides. The donors have opened up an agenda that at a very deep level is about moral standards and societal values. It is inappropriate to assume that western standards and values alone are important. Donor governments and the international financial institutions must, also, be willing to face the same questions about competence, transparency, accountability and legitimacy, as must international NGOs.

The logical conclusion of the mutual dependency of economic and political democracy is that the state has a critical role to play in managing economic affairs, in fostering gender equality and social justice for all marginalised groups, and in taking the steps necessary to ensure a more equitable distribution of resources, such as land and capital. In order to be able to fulfil this governance role, state structures and governments themselves need to be democratic, accountable, transparent, competent, and decentralised where appropriate. This democracy, accountability, transparency and competence, in turn, can only be secured by the presence of strong and participative political parties, women's organisations, community-based movements, workers' organisations, indigenous peoples' organisations and other social movements which can articulate their demands and ensure their satisfaction. This takes us right back to the four elements of the UK ODA's definition of good governance, but with the critical difference: a fundamentally redefined economic agenda.

Encouraging women to vote in South Africa's first ever full election, April 1994. Crossroads Township, Cape Town.
(Eric Miller/ Panos Pictures)

References

Ashworth, Georgina. (1994) 'Good Government, Bad Government, Participatory Democracy and Women', in Helen O'Connell and David Souter (eds). (1994), *Good Governance*, report of seminar on Good Governance, March 1994, London, One World Action, pp. 59–68.

Bowen, M. L. (1992) 'Beyond Reform: Adjustment and Political Power in Contemporary Mozambique', in *Journal of Modern African Studies*, No. 30, Vol. 2, Cambridge University Press.

Brittain, V. (1994) 'A State Remade to the United Nations Design', *The Guardian*, August 6, 1994.

Brittain, V. (1994) 'Absolute Minefield'. *The Weekend Guardian*, August 27, 1994.

Brochmann, G. and Ofstad A. (1990) *Mozambique: Norwegian Assistance in a Context of Crisis*, Bergen, Chr. Michelsen Institute.

Cariño, Joji. (1994) 'Challenges to Good Government Posed by Indigenous Peoples and Other Marginalised Groups', in Helen O'Connell and David Souter (eds). (1994), *Good Governance.*, report of seminar on Good Governance, March 1994, London, One World Action, pp. 35–45.

CEA/FEMNET. (1992) 'NGOs and women in Mozambique: a short paper', University of Mozambique, October.

Duckworth, Beverley. (1995) 'Gender, governance and accountability'. unpublished MA thesis, Institute of Development Studies, University of Sussex.

Elson, Diane. (1991) 'Gender and adjustment in the 1990s: an update on evidence and strategies', background paper for Inter-Regional Meeting on Economic Distress, Structural Adjustment and Women', June 13-14, Commonwealth Secretariat, London.

European Union. (1992) 'Declaration of the Council and of Representatives of Governments of Member States Meeting in the Council on Aspects of Development Cooperation Policy in the Run-up to 2000' (known as 'Horizon 2000'), Brussels.

European Union. (1992) *The Maastricht Treaty of the European Union*, Brussels.

Goodison, Paul. (1994) 'Good Governance and the European Union', in Helen O'Connell and David Souter (eds). (1994) *Good Governance*, report of seminar on Good Governance, March 1994, London, One World Action, pp. 51–53.

Hausermann, Julia. (1994) 'Good Governance and Human Rights: Two Sides of the Same Coin?', in Helen O'Connell and David Souter (eds). (1994) *Good Governance*, report of seminar on Good Governance, March 1994, London, One World Action, pp. 23–34.

Hermele, K. (1990) *Mozambican Crossroads: Economics and Politics in the Era of Adjustment*, Bergen, Chr. Michelsen Institute.

Jacobson, Ruth. (1994) *Dancing Towards a Better Future? Gender and the 1994 Mozambican Elections.* report prepared for the Norwegian International Cooperation Agency (NORAD), November.

Kanji, Nazreen. (1993) 'Gender and Structural Adjustment Policies: a Case Study of Harare', unpublished thesis.

Macquene, Althea and Pretorius, Leon. (1994) *Women's Formal Sector Employment and Trade Union Organisation*, London, One World Action.

Mengisteab, Kidane and Logan B. Ikubolajeh (eds)., (1995) *Beyond Economic Liberalization in Africa: Structural Adjustment and the Alternatives*, London and New Jersey, Zed Books.

Miller, M. (1993) 'Mozambique's Crisis of Governance: a Look at Population Displacement, Societal Change and Post-war State Capacity', M.Phil Dissertation, University of Cambridge, July.

Nyoni, Sithembiso. (1993) 'Economic Famine in Zimbabwe: the Impact of Economic Structural Adjustment Programme (ESAP) on Grassroots Development', unpublished paper.

O'Connell, Helen and Souter, David (eds). (1994) *Good Governance*, report of seminar on Good Governance, London, March 1994, London, One World Action.

Plank, D. N. (1993) 'Aid, Debt and the End of Sovereignty: Mozambique and its Donors', in *Journal of Modern African Studies*, Vol. 31, No. 3, pp. 407–430, Cambridge University Press.

Rahman, Atiur. (1994) 'The Sting in the Tail of Structural Adjustment Policies', paper prepared for Association of Development Agencies Bangladesh/One World Action consultation on structural adjustment, July 1994, Dhaka.

Saine, Abdoulaye S. M. (1995) 'Democracy in Africa: Constraints and Prospects' in Kidane Mengisteab and B. Ikubolajeh Logan (eds). (1995) *Beyond Economic Liberalization in Africa: structural adjustment and the alternatives*, London and New Jersey, Zed Books, pp. 182–198.
Stoneman, Colin. (1993) 'The World Bank: Some Lessons for South Africa', in *Review of African Political Economy*, No. 58, November 1993, Carfax Publishers for ROAPE Publications, Abingdon UK.

ODA (Overseas Development Administration). (1993) *Taking Account of Good Government*, Technical Note No. 10, London, ODA. (Reproduced in Helen O'Connell and David Souter (eds). (1994).)

Wapenhans, Willi A. (1992) *Effective Implementation: Key to Development Impact*, Washington, World Bank.

Woodroffe, Jessica. (1993) *Electricity in Ten Years Time — or Survival Now? Zimbabwe's structural adjustment programme*, London, Christian Aid.

World Bank. (1993) *Getting Results: the World Bank's Agenda for Improving Development Effectiveness*, Washington, World Bank.

ZCTU (Zimbabwe Congress of Trade Unions) . (1993) 'The Effects of Structural Adjustment on the Workforce in Zimbabwe', paper presented by Nicholas E. Mudzengerere, Acting Secretary General of ZCTU, to Winter School on the Social Implications of Economic Structural Adjustment Programmes in Southern Africa, University of Zimbabwe, June 7–22.

6. Finding New Balances

The dominant economic model is undemocratic and works against the interests of the majority of women, men and children. Countries in Latin America, Africa, Asia, in the Caribbean and Pacific, and now in Eastern and Central Europe are not free to choose their development path. The entire ethos of the economic model is to maximise and accumulate wealth, but not to distribute it more equally. The ethos is short-term and selfish. There is an unprecedented mobility of capital globally which can move finance within seconds, and can avoid economies with good labour or environmental codes. There is a massive concentration of control over resources, wealth and technology, and overconsumption by the majority in the North and a minority in the South. Everything, including many aspects of our lives, has become a commodity with a price tag. The arms trade is enormous and critically important to the economies of the North; this poses a fundamental problem few in power are willing to tackle. Poverty is increasing. Around 1.2 billion women, men and children live in desperate poverty; millions more are without the means to live with dignity, security and health each day.

The ground rules and realities of the economic model undermine the assumption, so strong in the Beijing Platform for Action and elsewhere, that somehow everything would be fine for all women, men and children if they could somehow have more opportunities and participate better in economic life. The strategy is to integrate poor countries into the global economy; in this way, the international community believes, poverty can be reduced. But the global economy is characterised by widening inequality and poverty. There is a similar strategy for women: integrate women into the 'mainstream' of social, economic and political life. A more equitable sharing of economic wealth, and the power that this brings with it, is a worthwhile objective, but the means of achieving it are increasingly questionable. Women cannot exercise and enjoy their full human rights in the context of mounting poverty and inequality (nor can men). Nor can development be sustainable as long as inequality is at its centre. Endorsing gender equality in order to achieve women's equal rights, and therefore sustainable people-centred development, can only be successful in practice if the dominant economic model and its inherently inequitable structures are transformed.

The role of aid in positively promoting long-term, equitable change in poor Southern countries is seriously in question. Aid, the development programmes and projects it funds, and the conditions attached to it, have become synonymous with increased hardship in many countries. Local organisations in the Philippines talk of large-scale economic development projects as 'development aggression'. In Bangladesh, Mozambique, Nicaragua and other countries, much aid and externally-defined development has become associated with increased poverty and abuse. There has been very little meaningful consultation with the women and men whose communities and rights are affected by development programmes and projects. There has been little compensation for lost resources and livelihoods.

There is a crisis in development thinking.

Given that sustainable poverty reduction is claimed as the overarching objective of the World Bank, most UN agencies and most bilateral donors, it is manifest that something fundamental is wrong with policy and practice.

Given that the election manifestos of most elected governments, South and North, contain some promises of improved well-being — more jobs, more services, less taxes — it is evident that here too rhetoric does not match reality.

The fact that most international non-governmental development organisations claim that they are working for the empowerment of the poor, and cite myriads of beneficial local-level projects in the midst of growing poverty, would seem to indicate that here too a change is long overdue.

A New Agenda

In the last 20 years, feminist organisations and networks have emerged alongside other broad social movements. They are taking the lead in questioning the dominant economic thinking and highlighting its failings. They are making the connections between what is happening in people's everyday lives and macro-level trends. They are putting their concerns on the political agenda.

Analysis of development policy and practice from a feminist and a gender perspective led many writers and activists from South and North to question the whole development model. Simply to press for women's greater participation in a system of development founded in gross inequalities between North and South, rich and poor, men and women, white and black, was seen as a flawed exercise. The debt crisis and the growing awareness of environmental destruction provided final proof, if proof were needed, that something fundamental was wrong. In June 1985, DAWN

(Development Alternatives with Women for a New Era), a group of Southern feminist academics and activists, published a radical critique, *Development, Crises and Alternative Visions: Third World Women's Perspectives* (Sen and Grown, 1985). The book set out DAWN's critique of the systemic crises facing the world and their vision and strategy for the future. Eleven years on, the evidence of systemic crises has grown and the thinking on alternatives has deepened.

We are consuming everything, BUT, you should be controlled. Poster of Narigrantha Prabartana, Bangladesh.

The decade from 1985 has seen the strengthening of international feminist movements on women's human rights, indigenous women's rights, reproductive rights, health, environment, science and technology, and economics. The cycle of UN conferences from Environment and Development in 1992 through to the Fourth World Conference on

Women in Beijing provided opportunities for activists from these networks to come together, exchange ideas and strategies, and lobby, successfully in very many cases, to ensure their issues and concerns were discussed.

The development paradigm and its economic underpinnings are under precise and detailed scrutiny. What is in question is not only development policy and practice in the South but economic policy and practice in the North. Feminist economists are exposing the male bias in orthodox economic theory and questioning the myths that markets are perfectly free, economics are gender-neutral and only work which is waged is economically productive. They are challenging the very core of patriarchal economic thinking and practice.

In recent years more and more voices have questioned the sustainability of the dominant economic model. People's protest movements are gaining influence and demanding policy changes; there are hundreds of local, national and international actions. Thinking on alternative development models is gaining ground and respectability even in official circles.

Economics for the Whole Economy
The economic experiences, choices, rewards and power of women and men are shaped by gender differences. Central to these differences are the sexual division of labour and the disproportionate share of family and household caring and maintenance roles carried by women. UNDP's 1995 *Human Development Report* estimated that US16,000 billion of global output is 'invisible' because it is unwaged or underwaged; US$11,000 billion of this work is done by women. For decades, activists and researchers have struggled to get unwaged work counted and valued. Unwaged work includes a vast range of activities: child care, cooking, cleaning, fetching water or fuelwood, caring for the elderly or ill, producing food, community work, environmental conservation. The classification of unwaged work as unproductive or non-market, and therefore valueless, is critical in national and international systems which to a great extent recognise only monetary or market values. It devalues vital areas of human activity — caring, nurturing, solidarity — and devalues those who do them, mainly women. Secondly, uncounted, unvalued and invisible work means uncounted, unvalued and invisible workers who have little claim on policy-makers' attention or support services. Putting a value on unwaged work for national accounting purposes gives this work visibility and economic status.

The Platform for Action agreed at the UN Fourth World Conference on Women in Beijing in September 1995 included an agreement to count and value unwaged work. It is an important step towards recognising the importance of this work, and towards ensuring that women's social and economic policy interests are recognised and satisfied, and it opens the way for a fundamental rethink of social policy. It opens the way, also, for the reorganisation of waged work to enable women and men to combine family and home and waged work responsibilities.

Changing the way in which reproductive work is regarded is only part of the economic transformation needed. Productive work — waged economic activities of all kinds — also need to be regarded differently. Diane Elson talks about the need for a 'dual emphasis' in order to achieve gender equality and human-centred development: 'It requires not just a transformation of the reproductive economy to facilitate women's participation in the productive economy but also a transformation of the productive economy to recognise the community and family responsibilities of both men and women. (Elson, 1995: 276)

There is a male bias in the development process which operates in favour of men as a gender and against women as a gender. This ill-founded and unjustified asymmetry in development policy is 'encouraged by male bias in every-day attitudes and practices and by male bias in analysis, reinforced by male bias in politics' (Elson, 1995: 11). The lack of explicit consideration of unequal gender relations means that, in practice, economic development strategies at all levels are biased in favour of men. This is true in export-led production, in agricultural development, in fisheries, in environmental management, in transport and in services and communications.

The economy is a highly gendered structure and has to be viewed and analysed as such. In this way only, can a social framework for gender equality and people-centred development be created. Economic systems to date — authoritarian, centrally-planned, and deregulated in line with the neo-liberal model — have all failed to provide the conditions for gender equality and people-centred development. Economics to date has dealt with parts only of economic and social life — those with a monetary value — and at the same time, because of its patriarchal form, it has exploited and devalued all the effort, energy, time and good will involved in reproducing and maintaining human resources — work not driven by economic self-interest. Elson argues that the best aspects of the process of reproduction and maintenance of human resources, which she suggests, are altruism, care, nurture, fellowship, empathy and solidarity, need to be incorporated into a framework for the whole economy. This can only be constructed, in her view, by 'an interlocking series of institutional changes at local, national and international levels' (Elson, 1995: 271).

Other areas of relations require transformation too. As with economic affairs, the political sphere is a highly gendered world and here, too, there is male bias. The daily social and economic decisions and actions concerned with family and community welfare, which are largely taken by women, are devalued and regarded as outside political affairs and of no consequence. All deliberations and decisions taken by village elders, local councils and national political structures, however informal or official, are deemed political; but each of these structures is patriarchal and hierarchical. Decisions are easily influenced by vested interest, patronage and personal gain.

Women in Black demonstrate about the use of violence against women as a tool of war in the former Yugoslavia. NGO Forum in Beijing during the Fourth World Conference on Women, September 1995. (Maya Mischke)

What is required is a transformation of official and informal political structures at local, national and international levels: firstly, to facilitate women's participation in the formal politics; secondly, to recognise the community and family responsibilities of both men and women; and thirdly, to recognise the international, national, local and personal responsibilities of governments and international institutions.

The agenda for change is enormous: gender relations, economics and politics, and needs to be seen as one. The international feminist movements and other progressive social movements refuse the compartmentalisation of issues which hides the connections between private and public, between unequal gender relations and economics and politics, between gender-based violence and patriarchal power. Those of us involved in these movements, and, particularly, feminist organisations, insist on the linkages between environment, development, population, human rights, poverty, gender equality and equity — the themes of the major UN conferences from 1992 to 1995. International feminist movements see organisation at local, national, regional and international level as the only way to bring about the transformation needed.

Women, and men, are taking action at every level, in communities, in local districts, nationally and internationally. Examples are plentiful but the following make the point.

Begnas, an alliance of women's groups from mining communities in the Cordillera region of the Philippines, is clear about its demands: protection and promotion of women's human rights, protection of their small-scale mining livelihoods from the destruction of large-scale open-caste mining, recognition of their rights to their ancestral lands. An international conference on women and mining in 1997 will bring women together from many countries, including the UK, to share experiences and strategies.

FETSALUD, the largest health workers' union in Nicaragua, convened a national assembly of 1,000 trade unionists in August 1993 to discuss and prepare a document on the basic conditions for reforms and principles for national health policies. Among their demands to the government were that it should decrease the prices of medicines; guarantee access to staple foods and ensure programmes for groups at risk; stop the implementation of direct cost recovery; stop the privatisation of services; guarantee the improvement of integral health care for women (not only contraceptive services); and guarantee the decentralisation of services to municipalities and health units. FETSALUD affirmed that it was willing to work with the government to bring about these changes.

In Bangladesh, community organisations take the lead in defending the National Drugs Policy, in providing education, health care, water services, credit, and cyclone protection. Community organisations in Angola, Mozambique, Zimbabwe and elsewhere work at local level trying to undo the damage done by wrong-headed neo-liberal economic policies.

What all these organisations, and thousands of others, have in common is a commitment to more equitable and just societies. What they also have in common is that, for the most part, their actions and opinions meet with disregard or condescension, and sometimes repression, from those in power.

There is action on other levels also. As we have seen, international feminist networks and others played a central role in the major UN conferences from 1992 to 1995. The Beijing Declaration and Platform for Action agreed at the UN Fourth World Conference on Women in September 1995 contain important statements on women's human rights and many recommendations for action by governments, international institutions and non-governmental organisations. Governments must now implement was what agreed and ensure that international institutions and NGOs act too.

The Maastricht Treaty of the European Union is clear that the objective of the EU's development cooperation is to reduce poverty, and to further democracy and respect for human rights. The EU's 1995 policy statement on structural adjustment (discussed in Chapter Three of this book) allows for a redefinition of economic reform programmes in ways which could lead to sustainable and equitable development. Its 1995 policy statement on integrating gender issues in development cooperation (discussed in Chapter One) commits the EU to reducing gender inequalities. While neither of these policy statements go far enough, and each regards development cooperation as separate both from other areas of Europe/South relations and Europe's own domestic affairs, their implementation is important and their very implementation will throw light on policy contradictions. The European Union is examining the coherence and consistency in its policies: external, internal, economic, agriculture, trade, development cooperation, gender equality, and so on. There is a long way to go before its commitment to gender equality, democracy and respect for human rights, in Europe and in the South, inform all its policy decisions. Coherence, between the well-being and interests of the poorest women and men, of indigenous peoples and other marginalised groups, and EU policies is even further away.

Macro-level economic decisions are taken outside the direct gaze of those whose lives are on the line — in the board rooms of transnational corporations and international finance companies, at the World Bank, IMF, at meetings of the Group of Seven, at the European Union Council of Ministers, at the World Trade Organisation, and at Davos. These must be brought into line with governments' stated commitments to gender equality, democracy, and respect for human rights.

International feminist networks and other social movements are putting the spotlight on these centres of power and the decisions taken there. This is a central focus of One World Action's work.

Action on Many Fronts
There is no blueprint, but there are social, economic and political choices. Gender equality requires systematic and

comprehensive action in every sphere: home, family, community, workplace, trade unions, board rooms, education, media, local and national legislatures, the judiciary, and international institutions and intergovernmental bodies. Aid could play a positive role at many levels.

Building and strengthening democracy at every level is a critical first step towards the transformation required for equitable and sustainable development. Open and active democracy is a valuable principle and an important tool; it is a valuable end in itself and also one way to achieve more equitable and sustainable development. Political rights which enable women and men to vote are important but insufficient on their own. Democracy needs to shape official politics — elections and legislative and executive decision-making — and, also, informal political, economic and social relations. Ways need to be found by which women's gender interests, local level community priorities and the views of minority groups are represented in decision-making structures, and by which decision-makers are held accountable and responsible for the decisions they take. Genuine consultation and public fora could play an important role. Transparency in decision-making is key, as is the role played by the media, education and literacy. It is possible to create spaces and structures which facilitate empowerment, rather than marginalisation. It is possible to close the gap between the lives, plans and priorities of women and men, and the mainstream policy agenda.

Other areas of political relations require change too. The notion of interdependence is strong and growing: understanding of the shared environment and its degradation has provided powerful stimulus. Telecommunications and mass media shrink the world. More and more people are embroiled in the globalising economy. Yet, the full ramifications of our interdependence are ignored by political leaders whose vision of interconnectedness seems to be determined by a narrow interpretation of national interest: the push to freer trade and deregulation, but also a fear of migration, fear of rising population numbers, fear of too much unrest in poor countries. It is time to adopt a much more holistic approach to international affairs. Mechanistic and short-term responses to conflict situations, be they civil wars, ethnic conflict or famine, fail to tackle the causes and fail to build the institutional foundations for long-term peace and stability.

Redefining economic development is another critical step. The long-term objectives of gender equality, more equitable distribution of wealth and resources, poverty reduction, greater security, and sustainable and responsible use and management of natural resources need to determine economic policy and practice. We have to find a new balance between production for local needs and for export. The new economic agenda needs to take a sensitive and sophisticated approach to trade liberalisation, privatisation and regulation and to be responsive to local and national differences. Obstacles to long-term economic development and well-being, such as male bias, and the debt burden, have to be removed. Investment in employment-intensive economic development is vital but integral to this has to be respect for workers' rights. The informal economy needs to be formalised in terms of investment in support and training, the application of labour standards, and revenue collection. Central to transforming the reproductive and productive economies, and the relationship between them, is exploring and developing ideas on the ways in which waged work is organised. There are many issues here: who is employed, how jobs are defined, hours worked, attitudes to leave, work-related entitlements.

A redefined economic agenda would give priority to investment in services, waged and unwaged, which strengthen and expand women's and men's capabilities to live with dignity, happiness and compassion. Village surveys and research, in which women's opinions on priorities are canvassed, South and North, invariably place health, education, housing and other basic services at the top of the list. These essentials are what people want most for their children and themselves.

The measure of success of the equitable economic agenda would not be quantitative growth in GNP but long-term improvements in the quality of the lives of women, men and children. UNDP's (1995) gender-related development index and its gender empowerment measure are valuable starting points.

Last, but by no means least in importance in achieving the transformation needed in social, economic and political structures, is the reorganisation and regulation of international institutions and other Northern government-dominated intergovernmental groupings. Democracy, responsibility, accountability and transparency are vital here. It is these institutions and groupings which have it within their power to reshape the international economy through international agreements, regulations and norms. They could regulate the operations of international finance and transnational corporations. They could control sex-trafficking and the trade in pornography, arms and narcotics. This reshaping of the international economy would support gender equality and people-centred development.

To postpone action on these fronts is to postpone equality between women and men, and to jeopardise our future well-being, security and peace.

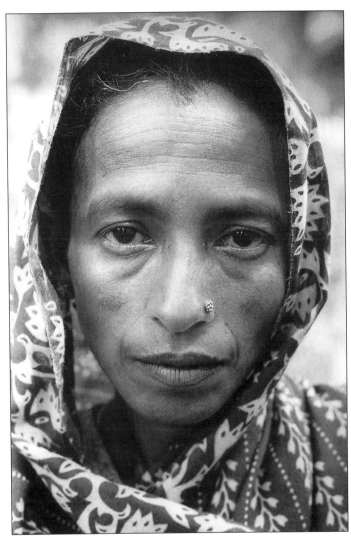

Shanti Bala runs a tree nursery on Moheshkhali Island in Cox's Bazaar in Bangladesh. The nursery was started by Gonoshasthaya Kendra. Women earn an income running the nursery and the trees provide women in the community with fruit, and fodder for their animals. The trees have the added benefit of strengthening the flood embankments.
(Jenny Matthews)

References

Elson, Diane (ed.). (1995 – second edition) *Male Bias in the Development Process*. Manchester, Manchester University Press.

Sen, Gita with Grown, Caren. (1985) *Development, Crises, and Alternative Visions: Third World Women's Perspectives*. Stavanger, Norway, DAWN (Development Alternatives with Women for a New Era).

UNDP. (1995) *Human Development Report 1995*. New York and Oxford, Oxford University Press.

Bibliography

Afshar, Haleh and Dennis, Carolyne (eds.). (1992) *Women, Recession and Adjustment in the Third World*, New York, St Martin's Press.

AMIHAN (National Federation of Peasant Women). (1992) `Their Failure Become Our Strength', Conference proceedings from Asian Peasant Women Dialogue on the General Agreement on Tariffs and Trade and Structural Adjustment Programs, Las Britas Hotel, Antipolo, Rizal, Philippines, 9-18 November 1992.

Anderson, Bridget. (1992) *Britain's Secret Slaves: an Investigation into the Plight of Overseas Domestic Workers*, London, Anti-Slavery International.

Ashworth, Georgina (ed.). (1996) 'What the Platform for Action Means to You... ' Report of January 20, 1996 conference of same name, January 20, 1996, London, Change.

Ashworth, Georgina. (1995) *The Diplomacy of the Oppressed: New Directions in International Feminism*, London and New Jersey, Zed Books.

Bakker, Isabella (ed.). (1994) *The Strategic Silence: Gender and Economic Policy*, London and New Jersey, Zed Books in association with The North-South Institute.

Bowen, M L. (1992) `Beyond Reform: Adjustment and Political Power in Contemporary Mozambique', in *The Journal of Modern African Studies*, No.30, Vol.2, Cambridge University Press.

Brennan, Brid, Vervest, Peitje and Heijmans, Erik. (1995) Asia's Wake up Call to Europe: the Perspectives for the Philippines. Papers for Transnational Institution conference, March 13-14, 1995, Amsterdam.

Brochmann, G. and Ofstad A. (1990) *Mozambique: Norwegian Assistance in a Context of Crisis*, Bergen, Chr. Michelsen Institute.

Butler, Judy. (1994) *The Emergency Social Investment Fund (FISE) in Nicaragua: an Evaluation*, London, One World Action.

Casimiro, Isabel, Laforte, Ana and Pessoa, Ana. (1991) *A Mulher em Moçambique*, Maputo,   Centro de Estudos Africanos.

CEAL (Centro de Estudios y Analysis Socio Laborales). (1994) *Nicaragua's Health Service Reforms 1990-1994*, London, One World Action.

Chant, Sylvia. (forthcoming 1996) 'Women's Roles in Recession and Economic Restructuring in Mexico and Philippines'. Draft for Alan Gilbert (ed.). (forthcoming 1996) *Poverty and Global Adjustment: the Urban Experience*, Oxford, Blackkwell.

Chant, Sylvia and McIlwaine, Cathy. (1994) 'Gender and Export Manufacturing in the Philippines: Continuity or Change in Female Employment? The Case of the Mactan Export Processing Zone', paper prepared for Gender Issues Panel, European Conference on Philippine Studies, School of Oriental and African Studies, University of London, April 13-15 1994.

Chari, Unity, A. (1993) *Positive Action Measures to Promote the Equality of Women in Employment in Zimbabwe*, Working paper from ILO Equality for women in employment: an interdepartmental project, Geneva, ILO, November.

Chowdhury, Zafrullah. (1995) *The Politics of Essential Drugs: the Makings of a Successful Health Strategy: Lessons from Bangladesh*, London and New Jersey, Zed Books.

CWERC (Cordillera Women's Education and Resource Center) and WWP (Women Workers Program). (1994) *Women Workers Situation at the Baguio City Export Processing Zone*, Baguio City, CWERC and WWP.

Dalla Costa, Mariarosa and Dalla Costa, Giovanna. (1995) *Paying the Price: Women and Politics of International Economic Strategy*, London and New Jersey. Zed Books.

Duckworth, Beverley. (1995) 'Gender, Governance and Accountability. unpublished MA thesis, Institute of Development Studies, University of Sussex.

Duza, Asfia and Begum, Hamida A. (1993) Emerging new accents: a perspective of gender and development in Bangladesh. Dhaka, Women for Women.

Elson, Diane (ed.). (1995 - second edition) *Male Bias in the Development Process*, Manchester, Manchester University Press.

European Union. (1995) 'Integrating Gender Issues in Development Cooperation'. Policy agreed at the Development Council of Ministers, December 20, 1995.

Evans, Trevor, Castro, Carlos and Jones, Jennifer. (1995) *Structural Adjustment and the Public Sector in Central America and the Caribbean*. Managua, CRIES (Coordinadora Regional de Investigaciones Economicas y Sociales).

Fleming, S. (1993) 'Women on the Sidelines: Policy and Poverty in Mozambique', Paper prepared for the African Studies Association of the UK one day meeting on Gender and adjustment in Africa, Liverpool, 14 September 1993.

Garfield, Richard and Williams, Glen . (1989) *Health and Revolution: the Nicaraguan Experience*, Oxford, Oxfam UK/Ireland.

Goetz, Anne Marie (ed.). (1995) *Getting Institutions Right for Women*, *IDS Bulletin* Vol. 26, No. 3, July 1995. Brighton, Institute of Development Studies.

Gibbon, P, Havnevik K. J, and Hermele, K. (1993) *A Blighted Harvest: the World Bank and African Agriculture in the 1980s*, London & New Jersey, James Currey & Africa World Press.

Harcourt, Wendy (ed.). (1994) *Feminist Perspectives on Sustainable Development*, London and New Jersey, Zed Books.

Hippler, Jochen (ed.). (1995) *The Democratisation of Disempowerment: the Problem of Democracy in the Third World*, London, Pluto Press with the Transnational Institute.

Jacobson, Ruth. (1994) 'Dancing Towards a Better Future? Gender and the 1994 Mozambican Elections', Report prepared for the Norwegian International Cooperation Agency (NORAD), November.

Jahan, Rounaq. (1995) *The Elusive Agenda: Mainstreaming Women in Development*, London and New Jersey, Zed Books.

Joekes, Susan and Weston, Ann. (1994) *Women and the New Decade Agenda*, New York, UNIFEM.

Kabeer, Naila. (1994) *Reversed Realities: Gender Hierarchies in Development Thought,* London and New York, Verso.

Low Pay Unit. (1994) *Out of Poverty, Towards Prosperity: a Report on Poverty, Low Pay and the Minimum Wage,* London, Low Pay Unit.

Macdonald, Mandy (ed.). (1994) *Gender Planning in Development Agencies: Meeting the Challenge,* Oxford, Oxfam UK/Ireland.

Macdonald, Mandy (ed.). (1995) *Women's Rights and Development: Vision and Strategy for the 21st Century.* Oxfam Discussion Paper 6. Report of seminar of same title organised by One World Action, Oxfam UK/Ireland, the Gender Institute of the London School of Economics, and Queen Elizabeth House University of Oxford, May 24, 1995.

Marshall, J. M. (1992) *War, Debt and Structural Adjustment in Mozambique,* Ottawa, The North-South Institute.

Mengisteab, Kidane and Logan, B Ikubolajeh (eds). (1995) *Beyond Economic Liberalization in Africa: Structural Adjustment and the Alternatives,* London and New Jersey, Zed Books.

Moore, Mick (ed.) (1993) *Good Government?* IDS Bullletin Vol. 24, No. 1, January 1993, Brighton, Institute of Development Studies.

Mosca, Joao and Delgado, Felisa Cena. (1993) 'Alguns Aspectos Sobre os Efectos do PRE na Agricultura'. Maputo, *Estudos Moçambicanos 13,* Centro de Estudos Africanos, May 1993, pp 53- 78.

Moser, Caroline (ed.). (1994) *Gender Planning and Development: Theory, Practice and Training,* London, Routledge.

O'Connell, Helen and Souter, David (eds.). (1994) *Good Governance,* Report of seminar on Good Governance, London March 1994. London, One World Action.

OECD Development Assistance Committee. (1995) 'Gender Equality: Moving Towards Sustainable, People-centred Development', Position agreed at a high level meeting, May 1995.

Ofreneo, Rene E. and Pineda-Ofreneo, Rosalinda. (1991) 'Filipino Workers in Japan: Caught in an Unequal Global Division ofLlabour', Paper presented at the symposium on

Japanese Economy and Migrant Workers from Abroad, October 12, 1991 at Kanagawa University, Yokohama, Japan.

One World Action. (1996) *Trade Unions and Development in a Changing Global Economy*, Report of One World Action seminar of same title, London, June 1995. London, One World Action.

Oppenheim, Carey and Harker, Lisa. (1996) *Poverty: the Facts*, London, Child Poverty Action Group.

Palma Beltran, Ruby and Javate de Dios, Aurora (eds). (1992) *Filipino Women Overseas Contract Workers ... At What Cost?*, Quezon City, Women in Development Foundation Inc. and Goodwill Trading Co. Limited,

Palmer, Ingrid. (1988) *Gender Issues in Structural Adjustment of sub-Saharan African Agriculture and Some Demographic Implications*, ILO World Employment Programme Research Working Paper, Geneva, ILO.

Pertierra, R. (ed.). (1992) *Remittances and Returnees: the Culture and Economy of Migration in Ilocos*, Quezon City, New Day Publishers.

Plank, D. N. (1993) 'Aid, Debt and the End of Sovereignty: Mozambique and its Donors', in *The Journal of Modern African Studies*, Vol. 31, No. 3, pp. 407-430, Cambridge University Press.

Raquiza, Ma. Victoria R. (1995) Women, Debt, Free Trade and the Paradox of Development in the Philippines, *Briefing Paper*, London, One World Action.

Reardon, Geraldine (ed.). (1995) *Power and Process: a Report from the Women's Linking for Change Conference, Thailand, 1994*, Oxford, Oxfam UK/Ireland.

Robinson, Mark (ed.). (1995) *Towards Democratic Governance*, IDS Bulletin, Vol. 26, No 2, April 1995. Brighton, Institute of Development Studies.

Sachs, Wolfgang (ed.). (1992) The Development Dictionary: a Guide to Knowledge as Power, London and New Jersey, Zed Books.

Sen, Gita with Grown, Caren. (1985) *Development, Crises, and Alternative Visions: Third World Women's Perspectives.*

Stavanger, Norway, DAWN (Development Alternatives with Women for a New Era).

Sparr, Pamela (ed.). (1994) *Mortgaging Women's Lives: Feminist Critiques of Structural Adjustment,* London and New Jersey, Zed Books.

Stoneman, Colin. (1993) 'The World Bank: Some Lessons for South Africa' in *Review of African Political Economy,* No 58, November 1993, Carfax Publishers for ROAPE Publications, Abingdon, UK.

UNDP. (1995) *Human Development Report 1995.* Oxford and New York, Oxford University Press.

United Nations. (1995) *The Beijing Declaration and Platform for Action.New York, United Nations.*

United Nations. (1991) *The World's Women: Trends and Statistics 1970-1990,* New York, United Nations.

United Nations. (1989) *Convention on the Elimination of All Forms of Discrimination Against Women.*

UK Overseas Development Administration. (1994) 'Women's Status in Developing Countries: British Aid and Human Rights Policy', Speech by Baroness Chalker, Minister for Overseas Development, November 2, 1994 at Queen Elizabeth House, Oxford.

Van Lieshout, Mary (ed.). (1996) *A Woman's World: Beyond the Headlines.* Dublin, Attic Press and Oxfam UK/Ireland.

Van Staveren, Irene. (1996) *The Gendered Economy.* Oegstgeest, The Netherlands, Vrouwenberaad Ontwikkelingssamenwerking.

Walker, Bridget M. and Dava, Gabriel L. (1994) *The Social Dimensions of Adjustment (SDA) Initiative in Mozambique: an Evaluation,* London, One World Action.

Wee, Vivienne and Heyzer, Noeleen. (1995) *Gender, Poverty and Sustainable Development: Towards a Holistic Framework of Understanding and Action,* Singapore, Centre for Environment, Gender and Development (ENGENDER).

Woestman, Lois. (1994) *World Bank Adjustment and Gender Policies: Strangers in the Night, Fleeting Acquaintances or Best Friends?,* Brussels, European Network on Debt and Development (EURODAD) and Network Women in Development Europe (WIDE).

Women Working Worldwide. (1991) *Common Interests: Women Organising in Global Electronics*, London, Women Working Worldwide.

Woodroffe, Jessica. (1993) *Electricity in Ten Years Time - or Survival Now? Zimbabwe's structural adjustment programme*, London, Christian Aid.

World Bank. (1993) *Getting Results: the World Bank's Agenda for Improving Development Effectiveness*, Washington, World Bank.

World Bank. (1994) *Enhancing Women's Participation in Economic Development*, a World Bank policy paper, Washington, World Bank.

Young, Kate. (1993) *Planning Development with Women: Making a World of Difference*, London and Basingstoke, Macmillan.

ONE WORLD ACTION

INCORPORATING THE NICARAGUA HEALTH FUND

One World Action is a partnership between the poor and exploited people in the South and those in the North who share their vision of a better, more equal world. We believe in taking bold, innovative steps to end poverty, inequality and discrimination, and support those who challenge the unequal distribution of the world's resources. One World Action supports local organisations in the countries of the South by giving money, goods, expertise and information as requested. We support non-governmental organisations, women's groups, trade unions, cooperatives, small farmer associations and community-based movements. What these groups have in common is a firm belief in democracy and equality linked with a respect for human rights and freedoms. Although our partner organisations are making waves of change throughout the South, we recognise that global indebtedness, environmental degradation and military conflict need to be addressed before poverty, injustice and inequality can finally be removed.

One World Action has an active education programme in Britain and the rest of Europe. We consider it a matter of urgency to bring to the attention of people in Europe the concerns of our partner organisations.

One World Action
5th Floor
Weddel House
13-14 West Smithfield
London EC1A 9HY
Tel: 0171 329 8111
Fax: 0171 329 6238
E-mail owa@gn.apc.org

Charity registration number: 1022298